SLOW COOKER RECIPES

Delicious Slow Cooker Recipes That Help You Lose Weight Fast

<u>Complete With</u>

<u>Nutrition Information</u>

Wendy Wilson

The information in the following pages is broadly considered to be a truthful and accurate account of facts and as such any inattention, use or misuse of the information in question by the reader will render any resulting actions solely under their purview. There are no scenarios in which the publisher or the original author of this work can be in any fashion deemed liable for any hardship or damages that may befall them after undertaking information described herein.

Additionally, the information in the following pages is intended only for informational purposes and should thus be thought of as universal. As befitting its nature, it is presented without assurance regarding its prolonged validity or interim quality. Trademarks mentioned are done without written consent and can in no way be considered an endorsement from the trademark holder.

Table of Contents

Introduction

I want to thank you and congratulate you for downloading my latest book, *"Slow Cooker Recipes: Delicious Slow Cooker Recipes That Help You Lose Weight Fast"*.

As a Chef, coming out with a cookbook is kind of easy but this book contains a selective list of recipes with Weight Watchers Smart points included and proven steps and strategies on how to prepare healthy, satisfying, and delicious meals that will help you reach your weight loss goals.

I've found losing weight, maintaining a healthy life and keeping fit have all become so much easier when you have a slow cooker in your kitchen. No matter how busy your daily schedule is, you can still enjoy healthy meals because with a slow cooker, all you have to do is throw together the ingredients in the pot, put it on the right settings, and leave it alone while you go about your day. If you are new to this I recommend to grab my other book at the end of this book

With the help of this cookbook and with a high quality slow cooker, you can prepare healthy dishes at home and be able to monitor the number of calories that you consume. Slow cooking will only require minimal kitchen time, and you can go about your day while the slow cooker prepares your meals for you.

The key to successfully losing weight is by combining exercise with your diet. Most important of all though is self-discipline. Start with these weight loss recipe meals and good luck reaching your goals!

Thanks again for downloading this book, I hope you enjoy it!

The Effective Weight Loss Method

Unlike many diet, the Weight Watchers diet allows you to eat anything you want like ice cream, pasta, cheese, and all your other favorite things while enabling you to lose weight. With the help of this diet, you'll learn how you can become healthier without sacrificing your love for food.

With the Weight Watchers diet, you'll learn how to create healthier food without taking away so much from the taste department. In the following chapters, you'll learn how you can cook flavorful soup, fulfilling main dishes, yummy salad and side dishes, loaded breakfast and appetizers, and delicious desserts.

The Weight Watchers diet prevents you from taking in empty calories without worrying too much on what you eat. It takes minimal effort to follow this diet as all you have to do is to follow the recipes I've included in this book. If you want to take the diet to the next level, you can also search online for personalized activity goals to help you reach your weight goals faster.

Aside from exercise and diet plans, you can also find communities online who can give you advice and tips so you can also be successful in this diet. You can also let your family join in on the fun as this diet is good for everybody.

People with high cholesterol, diabetes, high blood pressure, and heart disease will especially benefit from this diet as it helps you maintain healthy levels of food nutrition to prevent complications caused by improper diet. If you're having second thoughts, you can always check with your doctor whether this type of diet will affect your health.

In the next chapters, you will learn more than a hundred Weight Watchers recipes that you can use to spice up your meal plan or to entice a loved one to join you in this healthier food lifestyle.

Smart Points Explain

In 2016, Weight Watchers announced that they are moving to a new program, "Beyond the Scale" and with that, the points system will also change. Weight Watchers is moving from the old points system of Points Plus to a new and healthier points system, "Smart Points".

With Smart Points, food items that are higher in saturated fat and/or sugar are higher in Smart Points' values. Food items that have high lean protein are scored lower in Smart Points' values. As you can see, you are directed towards healthier choices.

- Every food is allocated its own Smart Points value based on four components: saturated fat, calories, protein, and sugar.

- Protein lowers the Smart Points values.

- Sugar and saturated fat surge the Smart Points values.

In nutshell, it rewards you for eating less sugar and saturated fat, and more lean protein.

Another important change in the new point systems is that FitPoints® have replaced Activity Points and the new points are calculated based on different kinds of activities ranging from daily chores to more planned exercise.

Under the Points Plus approach, you were given 49 weekly points to use however you wanted. In the Smart Points approach, this number will be adjusted based on your weight loss goals, activity level, gender, age, and other factors.

Smart Points Good And Bad

As you know any new system has its pros and cons and it's really important for you to be aware of both so that you can take the informed decision. Let's have a quick look at some of the pros and cons of using the Smart Points approach:

Pros

- Smart Points main objective is to close all the loopholes that exist within the Points Plus approach. For example, the Point Plus approach use to encourage people to eat foods that are loaded with sugars and other additives. This made them taste as good as full-fat foods.

- Under the Point Plus approach, if you are doing exercise, you can earn more points that you can spend on food. In nutshell, if you want to eat more, exercise more. This leads to an unhealthy mindset about food and how it should be used to fuel your body. Under the new Smart Points approach, you can no longer trade your exercise points with food. In nutshell, the new system separates your food intake and the activity.

- The new Smart Points system is more about creating an overall healthier lifestyle and less about weight loss. Whereas, the Points Plus system use to focus on counting calories. The Smart Points encourages you to choose the foods with the least sugar and most protein, which is a healthier choice for a healthier lifestyle.

Cons

- For many experienced Weight Watchers, the biggest drawback is to get used to the new system, especially, when they have enjoyed success with Points Plus. These members can still use the Points Plus system, but to be honest; Weight Watchers will definitely phase it out.

- Many people claim that the Points Plus use to provide them amazing freedom and flexibility, which might not be the case with Smart Points as it pushes some of the foods away for the others.

- Eating sugar and saturated fat will have higher penalties than the Points Plus system. Some Weight Watchers members believe that the penalties for cookies and cake are now so high that it might cause some members to go off-plan and eat the foods that might affect their will power.

Smart Points Calculator

It's worthwhile to note that over 50% of the Points Plus points will be changed when you move to Smart Points. Foods with lean proteins will quickly lower your point's value. You will also love the fact that now lean meats, for example, prawns, turkey, and most seafood will have just 1 Smart Points, while chicken will drop to just 2 Smart Points (which use to worth 3 Points Plus earlier).

Points on dairy products have gone up even if it's 'non-fat' or 'low-fat'. Sugar is also a strictly no-no area as, now, one tablespoon of granulated white sugar will have up to 3 Smart Points which use to be 1 under the Points Plus approach. This will be a huge change for people who like a piece of chocolate or sugar in their tea.

Fruits and vegetables will remain point-free but with one important change: fruits included in other recipes will now be free too.

Here is the rough Smart Points food value calculation:

(Calories * .0305) + (Sat Fat * .275) + (Sugar * .12) - (Protein * .098)

For example, if a food item has the following nutritional value:

Calories; 330, Protein 2g, Carbohydrate 70g, Fiber 0g, Total Fat 5g, Saturated Fat 3g, and sugar 57g

The Smart Points value would be:

(330 Cal * .0305) + (3g fat * .275) + (57g sugar * .12) - (2g Protein * .098) = 18 smart points

Tips for getting your diet goal

Even if you are armed with the best recipes, there are certain habits that you must adopt if your diet is going to be a success. Some of these are lifestyle adjustments; others are about shifting your thought patterns or changing lifelong bad habits. If you are part of a weight loss support group, you likely already have an arsenal of tips for success, but this is one area that you can never have too much of. Here are a few simple tips for long term success with your healthy eating and weight loss goals.

1. Drink more water. It is impossible to be your healthiest self if you are not properly hydrated. Water is vital for practically every function of your body. Plus, sometimes hunger cues are really just your body telling you that you are thirsty. Keep a glass or bottle of water with you throughout the day to quench thirst and fight off unnecessary cravings.

2. Divide foods up into smaller portion sizes as soon as you get home from the grocery store, preferably when you are not hungry. Foods such as cheese or nuts are nutritious, but also calorie dense and very easy to overindulge in. On the other hand, cut up vegetables offer a low calorie, healthy option that will fill you up. When you open up your refrigerator to reach for a snack, go ahead and have the cheese, just grab one of the small snacking portions that you have prepared. You might also look at the entire bowl of salad that you can have instead and choose the more filling option.

3. Add exciting new life to your favorite foods by adding different herbs. If you have always wanted to try a herb, but never had the occasion to do so, now is the time. Choose fresh herbs whenever possible. They pack more of a flavor punch and on an emotional level feel more indulgent. Some herbs are more potent than others, so it is best to do some preliminary research online to know which herbs you should use in moderation.

4. Listen to your body. Think about all of the times that your body leads you in the right direction if you are willing to trust it. A toddler will binge on fruit when they need vitamin C. A pregnant woman might crave steak if she needs iron. If you are craving

something sweet, don't just shrug that craving aside, but modify how you satisfy the urge. Instead of ice cream, choose a nondairy alternative. Instead of cherry pie, indulge in a bowl of berries with a little bit of whipped topping and nut crumble. Instead of the chocolate cake, sit down with a rich piece of dark chocolate and savor the intensity of the flavor. Do this with all of your cravings that can be classified as "unhealthy".

5. Portion control is crucial. Learn to recognize what three ounces of meat or one cup of pasta looks like. Invest in a food scale and accurate measuring utensils and measure everything, especially until you feel that you can recognize an appropriately sized portion.

6. Start with small steps. Begin by adding a healthy portion of vegetables to your lunch time sandwich. Next time, scale back a little on the meat or cheese. After that, trade out fattening condiments such as mayo for mustard, etc. We are trained to resist too much change, which is a trap for losing control of your diet. Making small little changes that eventually lead up to big ones will help to ensure long term success.

7. Make it a goal to try one new healthy food or recipe each week. This will give you something to look forward to and expand the diversity of your options.

8. Make meal or snack time a priority. This means shutting out all other distractions and not multitasking. Don't eat at your desk while you are working. Turn off your phone when you sit down for the family dinner and don't eat in front of the television. Being distracted and multitasking takes away from the pleasurable experience of eating and can result in consuming more calories throughout the day.

9. If you are having a hard time giving up a "forbidden" food, try to come up with an alternative. If you love mayonnaise, there are plenty of low-fat options available. If you crave fruit flavored sodas, try a sparkling water with a little fruit juice or fresh fruit added.

10. Speak up for yourself. Some people make sticking to your goals more difficult. Sometimes it is intentional, while other times people are well meaning, but uninformed. You cannot expect anyone to respect your goals if you do not make them known and let people know explicitly what is or isn't helpful. Tell grandmother that you love her cookies, but will not have more than one. Tell your coworkers that you cannot join them for lunch if they choose a place that doesn't offer any healthy alternatives, etc.

11. Brush your teeth often. Make a point of brushing your teeth after every meal, and even between meals to help fight off cravings. The mint flavor of toothpaste or mouthwash will help to signal a message to your brain that you are finished eating and are no longer hungry. Additionally, once you brush your teeth, it takes a while for most foods to taste good again. By the time the mouthwash has worn off, your cravings will be under control.

Slow Cooker Tips To Make Life Easier

If you are a veteran slow cooker user, then you likely know all the little nuances that come with this incredible appliance. However, some of you will pick up this book and a new slow cooker at the same time. You have made a wonderful choice. You will be amazed at how easy it is to prepare food that is nutritious and pleasing to your taste buds as well as your scale. Following are just a few tips to help you get started in slow cooking.

Not all slow cookers are the same.

Do a little research and find one that fits your needs, as well as one that has good customer reviews. Some slow cookers have a simple "LOW" and "HIGH" setting. Others will have more choices in temperature range and timing options. The recipes in this book have been designed to work with the most basic of slow cookers; however, if you plan on using your slow cooker quite often you might want to look into one with a little more variability. Also, consider size. Ask yourself questions like how big is your kitchen, will you keep it out when it is not in use or will you store it, how big is your family, how much food will you cook at once, are you looking to make extra and freeze it for later, etc.... Slow cookers come in various sizes. The recipes in this book have been created for use in five to seven-quart slow cookers, or larger.

Just because you throw it all in one pot, that doesn't mean it will all cook evenly.

You want as even cooking over the duration of the cooking period as possible. This means that foods that are cut, such as vegetables, should be cut according to cooking time. For example, a quicker cooking vegetable should be cut into larger pieces while slower cooking vegetables should be cut into smaller pieces. Some ingredients, such as peas or spinach, cook quickly enough that many times they can be added near the end of the cooking time to avoid them becoming too mushy or disintegrating completely during the cooking process.

Keep food safety in mind.

Cooking times given should be considered to be approximate, not set in stone. Your food might be thicker or cut in a different way, and your slow cooker might cook at a slightly different temperature than other models. Just like some ovens cook differently, so do slow cookers. For this reason, a good quality food thermometer is a good investment. As a general rule, you want meats to register at 165°F, especially for poultry. Cook beef according to temperature preferences, but use caution when handling beef that is more on the rare side.

Placement is key.

You will notice that in some of the recipes, the meat is placed on the bottom with the vegetables on top or surrounding the meat. In other recipes, the order is reversed. Sometimes a sauce is added first, sometimes it is added last. There really is a reason for the method, and it is all about what the final product will be. Generally, you want meats close to the bottom, so they have more exposure to the heat source since they typically take longer to cook. There are some recipes though, that depend on the juices of the meat dripping down over the vegetables for a specific flavor or texture.

A little moisture is good thing.

You do not need to drench each dish with cups of liquid, but it is always a good idea to add at least half a cup of liquid to the slow cooker. This will help prevent dryness or burning.

Not all foods make for a good slow cooker meal.

Fish and seafood can be cooked in a slow cooker, but require a much, much lower cooking time. Where beef or chicken might take four to eight hours, shrimp would take an hour or less. Many people find that the convenience of the slow cooker lies in the fill-it-and-leave-it-for-hours method. This doesn't really apply to fish and seafood. Don't get me wrong – you can create delicious seafood dishes in a slow cooker, it just takes a different approach. Another type of ingredient that doesn't do well in slow cookers is dairy. You can get away with a little dairy, but adding a significant quantity of dairy and leaving it in the slow cooker for hours will often result in a broken, curdled mess. When using dairy in your dishes, try adding it towards the end of cooking time for better results.

Slow Cooker Recipes

Breakfast Meal

Apple Cinnamon Oatmeal:

Serving Size: 1 cup

Servings per Recipe: 2

Smart Points per Serving: 7

Calories: 205

Cooking Time: 8 Hours

Ingredients:

- A cup outdated oats

- 1/2 teaspoon ground cinnamon

- 1/2 teaspoon vanilla concentrate

- Salt to taste

- 2 cups water to fill Slow Cooker around 1/4 of the way full

- 1/2 little apple, slashed

- Foul sweetener of decision, to taste

Nutrition Information:

- ✓ Saturated Fat: 0.5 g

- ✓ Cholesterol: 0 mg

- ✓ Sodium: 170 mg

- ✓ Carbohydrates: 27 g

✓ Dietary Fiber: 3 g

✓ Sugars: 12 g

✓ Protein: 3 g

Directions:

1. In a small oven-proof bowl, blend together oats, cinnamon, vanilla, and salt.

2. The apples can likewise be included here.

3. Pour two cups water over oats.

4. Fill Slow Cooker around 1/4 to 1/2 of the path full with water (this will rely on upon the span of your Slow Cooker).

5. Include the heatproof bowl with the oat blend to the slow cooker.

6. The bowl with the oats/cinnamon/vanilla has water in it and furthermore sits in the slow cooker encompassed by water.

7. The water level ought to rise practically to the highest point of the bowl.

8. Turn Slow Cooker on low for 7-8 hours overnight. Utilizing a huge spoon, expel bowl from Slow Cooker.

9. Mix in slashed apple and sweetener of choice.

Fresh Breakfast Omelets

Smart Points: 3

Servings: 2

Nutritional Info (per serving):

✓ Calories 110
✓ Sodium 436 mg
✓ Carbohydrates 1 g
✓ Total Fat 6 g

- ✓ Saturated Fat 2 g
- ✓ Cholesterol 213 mg
- ✓ Protein 12 g
- ✓ Calcium 29 mg

Ingredients:

- 2 eggs, plus 3 egg whites

- 1/2 teaspoon of olive oil

- 1/4 teaspoon each of salt and ground pepper

- 1 tablespoon of water

Directions:

1. In a bowl, beat the eggs, egg whites, salt, pepper, and water until frothy.
2. Heat half of the oil in a skillet over medium heat. Pour half of the egg mixture.
3. Cook for a couple of minutes, while lifting the edges using a spatula every once in a while. Fold into a half.
4. Turn the heat to low and continue cooking for a minute.
5. Repeat the process for the rest of the egg mixture.

Slow Cook Red Potato Frittata

Smart Points: 7

Servings: 4

Nutritional Info (1/4 of the recipe):

- ✓ Calories 273
- ✓ Sodium 491 mg
- ✓ Carbohydrates 30 g
- ✓ Total Fat 11 g
- ✓ Saturated Fat 5 g
- ✓ Cholesterol 203 mg

✓ Protein 16 g
✓ Calcium 172 mg

Ingredients:

- 4 eggs, plus 4 egg whites

- 3 small red potatoes (thinly sliced)

- 4 scallions (thinly sliced)

- 1/2 cup of low-fat (1%) milk

- 1 tablespoon of unsalted butter

- 1/4 teaspoon of ground pepper

- 1/4 cup of shredded fontina cheese

- 1/2 teaspoon of salt

- 2 teaspoons of minced fresh thyme (or 1/2 teaspoon of dried)

Directions:

1. Put the milk, eggs, egg whites, cheese, and thyme in a bowl. Mix until well-combined. Set aside.

2. Spray a skillet with a nonstick spray. Set it over medium heat. Put the potatoes, and season with salt and pepper. Cook for 8 minutes while stirring occasionally. Transfer to a plate.

3. Melt the butter in the same skillet over medium-low heat. Cook for 10 minutes or until the bottom is firm.

4. Put the skillet in a preheated broiler and broil it 5 inches from the heat. Do this for 5 minutes or until the center of the frittata is firm. Slice into 4 and serve while hot.

Tomato and Spinach Quiche

Smart Points: 7

Servings: 6

Nutritional Info (1/6 of the quiche): Calories 279, Sodium 571 mg, Carbohydrates 38 g, Total Fat 9 g, Saturated Fat 3 g, Cholesterol 80 mg, Protein 14 g, Calcium 250 mg, Fiber 3 g

Ingredients:

- 2 eggs, plus 1 egg white (lightly beaten)
- 3 medium onions (chopped)
- 3/4 cup of evaporated fat-free milk
- 1 10-ounce package of refrigerated pizza dough
- 1 10-ounce package of frozen chopped spinach (thawed and squeezed dry)
- 2 teaspoons of extra-virgin olive oil
- 1 teaspoon of sugar
- 1/8 teaspoon each of freshly ground pepper and nutmeg
- 1/2 teaspoon of salt
- 1/2 cup shredded reduced-fat Monterey Jack cheese
- 12 cherry tomatoes (halved)
- 2 garlic cloves (minced)
- 1/4 cup of light sour cream

Directions:

1. Heat oil in a skillet over medium heat. Put the garlic, onions, and sugar. Cook for 10 minutes while stirring occasionally. Put the spinach and cook

for a couple of minutes. Remove from the stove. Allow to cool for 10 minutes.

2. Spread the dough on a floured surface. Shape it into 4-inch round. Loosely cover with plastic and leave for 10 minutes. Roll the dough and fit it into a pie plate. Fold the edges.

3. In a bowl, whisk the eggs, egg white, milk, salt, pepper, nutmeg, and sour cream.

4. Sprinkle the cheese all over the crust. Follow it with the spinach mixture and add the egg mixture. Place the tomato halves with the cut part facing side up. Bake in a preheated oven at 350 degrees for 45 minutes.

5. Allow to cool for 10 minutes before slicing.

Ham and Mushroom Crêpes

Smart Points: 5

Servings: 6

Nutritional Info (1 crêpe with filling): Calories 203, Sodium 743 mg, Carbohydrates 19 g, Total Fat 7 g, Saturated Fat 3 g, Cholesterol 87 mg, Protein 16 g, Calcium 216 mg, Fiber 1 g

Ingredients:

- 2 eggs

- 1/2 cup of all-purpose flour

- 3/4 cup of low-fat (1%) milk

- 1/4 teaspoon of salt

For the filling

- 5 tablespoons of dry sherry

- 3/4 cup each of reduced-sodium chicken broth and low-fat (1%) milk

- Freshly ground pepper

- 3 tablespoons of all-purpose flour

- 1/2 cup freshly grated Parmesan cheese

- 2 cups of cremini mushrooms (sliced)

- 3 garlic cloves (minced)

- 2 tablespoons of parsley (chopped)

- 6 slices of deli-sliced cooked lean ham

- 1/4 teaspoon of salt

- 1/8 teaspoon each of cayenne and nutmeg

Directions:

1. Make the crêpes. Combine the salt and flour in a bowl. In another bowl, whisk the eggs and milk. Gradually combine the two mixtures until smooth. Leave for 15 minutes.

2. Spray a skillet with non-stick cooking spray and put over medium heat. Stir the batter a little. Pour 1/4 of the batter into the skillet. Tilt the skillet to form a thin and even crêpe. Cook for a couple of minutes or until the bottom is golden and the top is set. Flip and cook for 20 seconds. Transfer to a plate.

3. Repeat the steps with the remaining batter. Loosely cover the cooked crêpes with plastic wrap.

4. Make the filling. Put the following in a saucepan over medium heat – flour, milk, cayenne, nutmeg, pepper, and 3 tablespoons of sherry. Constantly whisk until thick or around 7 minutes. Remove from the stove. Stir in a tablespoon of parsley and cheese. Loosely cover to keep warm.

5. Spray a skillet with non-stick cooking spray and put over medium heat. Cook the garlic and mushrooms. Season with salt. Cook for 6 minutes or until the mushrooms are soft. Add 2 tablespoons of sherry. Cook for a couple of minutes. Remove from the stove. Add the remaining parsley and stir.

6. Put the crêpes side by side on a flat surface. Put a slice of ham in the middle of each piece. Spread a tablespoon of the sauce and 2 tablespoons of the cooked mushrooms. Roll up the crêpes and transfer them to a greased baking dish. Pour the rest of the sauce on top. Bake in a preheated oven at 450 degrees for 15 minutes.

Granola Fruits and Nuts

Smart Points: 8

Servings: 12

Nutritional Info (per 1/2 cup serving): Calories 296, Sodium 54 mg, Carbohydrates 52 g, Total Fat 8 g, Saturated Fat 1 g, Cholesterol 0 mg, Protein 7 g, Calcium 48 mg, Fiber 5 g

Ingredients:

- 1 cup each of dried cranberries and golden raisins

- 6 tablespoons of maple syrup

- 4 cups of old-fashioned rolled oats

- 2 tablespoons each of canola oil and warm water

- 1 teaspoon each of vanilla extract and cinnamon

- 1/4 cup of sesame seeds

- 1/4 teaspoon of salt

- 1/3 cup of honey

- 1/2 cup of slivered almonds

- 1/8 teaspoon of nutmeg

Directions:

1. In a bowl, mix the sesame seeds, nutmeg, almonds, oats, salt, and cinnamon.

2. In another bowl, mix the oil, water, vanilla, honey, and syrup. Gradually pour the mixture into the oats mixture. Toss to combine. Spread the mixture into a greased jelly-roll pan. Bake in a preheated oven at 300 degrees for 55 minutes. Stir and break the clumps every 10 minutes.

3. Once you get it from the oven, stir the cranberries and raisins. Allow to cool. This will last for a week when stored in an airtight container and up to a month when stored in the fridge.

French Toast

Smart Points: 3

Servings: 2

Nutritional Info (1 slice): Calories 131, Sodium 244 mg, Carbohydrates 15 g, Total Fat 4 g, Saturated Fat 1 g, Cholesterol 107 mg, Protein 10 g, Calcium 55 mg, Fiber 2 g

Ingredients:

- 1 egg, plus 2 egg whites

- 2 slices of firm whole wheat bread

- A pinch of cinnamon

- 2 tablespoons of fat-free milk

- 1/4 teaspoon of vanilla extract

Directions:

1. In a shallow dish, beat the milk, cinnamon, vanilla, egg, and egg whites. Soak each slice of bread into the mixture.

2. Grease a skillet with a butter-flavored non-stick spray over medium heat. Once hot, cook the bread slices until both sides are golden brown. Cook each side for about 3 minutes.

Add 1 Smart Point when you serve each slice with 1 ounce of Canadian bacon or top the slices with fresh strawberries and drizzle with a tablespoon of maple syrup.

Piña Colada Smoothie

Smart Points: 3

Servings: 4

Nutritional Info (per 1 cup serving): Calories 115, Sodium 93 mg, Carbohydrates 24 g, Total Fat 2 g, Saturated Fat 1 g, Cholesterol 2 mg, Protein 3 g, Calcium 90 mg, Fiber 1 g

Ingredients:

- 1 cup coconut water

- 1 cup of low-fat vanilla yogurt (frozen)

- 1 cup of ice cubes

- 1 cup of crushed pineapple in juice (drained)

- 1/2 cup of pineapple juice

Directions:

1. Chill the pineapple for at least 3 hours. Thaw at a room temperature for 10 minutes. Put in a blender, along with the ice cubes, coconut water, frozen yogurt, and pineapple juice. Process until smooth. Serve and enjoy.

Mango-Soy Smoothie

Smart Points: 3

Servings: 4

Nutritional Info (per 1 cup serving): Calories 101, Sodium 8 mg, Carbohydrates 25 g, Total Fat 0 g, Saturated Fat 0 g, Cholesterol 0 mg, Protein 2 g, Calcium 110 mg, Fiber 2 g

Ingredients:

- 1 cup of cubed mango
- 1 cup of ice cubes
- 1 tablespoon of sugar
- 1 cup of vanilla-flavored soy drink (chilled)
- 1 tablespoon of sweetened lime juice
- 3/4 cup of mango nectar

Directions:

1. Put the ice cubes in a blender. Process until crushed. Add the rest of the ingredients. Blend until smooth.

Slow Cook Savory Mexican Oats:

Serving Size: 1/2 cup

Servings per Recipe: 4

Smart Points per Serving: 3

Calories: 86

Cooking Time: 4 Hours

Ingredients:

- 1 cup steel cut oats
- 1 cup salsa
- 2 tablespoons new cilantro, cleaved
- 2-1/2 cups low sodium chicken soup, no sugar included
- 1 cup solidified corn, defrosted
- 1 cup red pepper, finely chopped

Nutrition Information:

- ✓ Saturated Fat: 0 g
- ✓ Cholesterol: 2 mg
- ✓ Sodium: 0 mg
- ✓ Carbohydrates: 16 g
- ✓ Fiber: 2 g
- ✓ Sugars: 2 g
- ✓ Protein: 3 g

Directions:

Mix everything together and let it cook for 3 to 4 hours at low temperature.

Maple Hazelnut Oatmeal:

Serving Size: 1-1/2 cup

Servings per Recipe: 4

Smart Points per Serving: 12

Calories: 358

Cooking Time: Approx. 7 Hours

Ingredients:

- 1/2 cups low-fat milk
- ½ cups water
- Cooking shower /spray
- 2 Gala apples, peeled and cut into 1/2-inch solid shapes (around 3 cups)
- 1 glass uncooked steel-cut oats
- 2 tablespoons cocoa sugar
- 1/2 tablespoons margarine, mellowed
- 1/4 teaspoon ground cinnamon
- 1/4 teaspoon salt
- 1/4 glass maple syrup
- 2 tablespoons hazelnuts, chopped

Nutrition Information:

- ✓ Saturated Fat: 4g
- ✓ Cholesterol: 13mg
- ✓ Sodium: 226mg
- ✓ Total Carbohydrate: 62g
- ✓ Dietary Fiber: 5g

✓ Protein: 9g

Directions:

1. Bring milk and 1/2 mugs water to the point of boiling in a pot over medium-high warmth, blending oftentimes.

2. Coat a 3 1/2-quart electric moderate cooker with a cooking splash.

3. Put hot milk batter, apple, and next 5 fixings in moderate cooker; mix well.

4. Cover and cook on low for 7 hours or until oats are delicate.

5. Spoon cereal into dishes; beat with maple syrup and hazelnuts.

Crock Pot Apple Granola Crumble:

Serving Size: 1-1/2 cup

Servings per Recipe: 4

Smart Points per Serving: 7

Calories: 180

Cooking Time: 4 Hours and 15 minutes

Ingredients:

- 2 green apples

- 1 measure of your most loved granola grain (you can blend two or types of granola if you wish to)

- 1/8 cup maple syrup

- 1/4 cup squeezed apple

- 2 tablespoons dairy free spread
- 1 teaspoon ground cinnamon
- 1/2 teaspoon ground nutmeg

Nutrition Information:

- ✓ Total Fat: 5g
- ✓ Cholesterol: 0mg
- ✓ Sodium: 135mg
- ✓ Carbohydrate: 31g
- ✓ Dietary Fiber: 5g
- ✓ Sugar: 11g
- ✓ Protein: 5g

Directions:

1. Peel, center and cut the apples into thick cuts and afterward lumps.

2. Slice the apple down the middle - then half again and after that those parts in halves as well.

3. This gives you 8 thick cuts. Cut those thick cuts in lumps around 3 for every cut.

4. Add everything to the slow cooker and blend well.

5. Cover and cook on low 4 hours.

Slow Cook Apple Pie Oatmeal:

Serving Size: 1

Servings per Recipe: 5

Smart Points per Serving: 7

Calories: 180

Cooking Time: Approx. 8 Hours

Ingredients:

- 1 cup of Steel-Cut Oats (ensured without gluten if vital)
- 4 cups of unsweetened Almond Milk (ensured without gluten if vital)
- 2 medium Apples, slashed
- 1 teaspoon Coconut Oil
- 1 teaspoon Cinnamon
- 1/4 teaspoon Nutmeg
- 2 tablespoon Maple Syrup
- Sprinkle of Lemon Juice

Nutrition Information:

- ✓ Total Fat: 5g
- ✓ Cholesterol: 0mg
- ✓ Sodium: 135mg

- ✓ Carbohydrate: 31g
- ✓ Dietary Fiber: 5g
- ✓ Sugar: 11g
- ✓ Protein: 5g
- ✓ Potassium: 109mg
- ✓ Iron: 8%
- ✓ Vitamin A: 9%
- ✓ Vitamin C: 6%
- ✓ Calcium: 40%

Directions:

1. Add all the ingredients to your cooking pan. Mix them well by stirring.

2. Cook on low flame for 8 hours or on high flame for 4 hours.

3. Give it a decent stir. Add toppings of your most loved garnishes. Such as peanut butter or crunched up apples.

4. Stash leftovers in the freezer for up to a week.

5. To warm the food, include a sprinkle of almond milk and reheat in the microwave or stove.

<u>Bacon, Egg & Hash Brown Casserole:</u>

Serving Size: 1 cup

Servings per Recipe: 8

Smart Points per Serving: 11

Calories: 342

Cooking Time: Approx. 4 to 8 Hours

Ingredients:

- 20-ounce pack solidified hash
- 8 cuts thick-cut bacon, cooked and coarsely slashed
- 8 ounces destroyed cheddar
- 6 green onions, cut thin
- 12 eggs
- 1/2 glass drain
- 1/2 teaspoon salt
- 1/4 teaspoon pepper
- Cooking oil

Nutrition Information:

- ✓ Total Fat: 22g
- ✓ Sodium: 648mg
- ✓ Carbohydrate: 14g
- ✓ Dietary Fiber: 2g
- ✓ Sugar: 2g
- ✓ Protein: 21g
- ✓ Potassium: 472mg
- ✓ Iron: 12%

- ✓ Vitamin A: 21%
- ✓ Vitamin C: 14%
- ✓ Calcium: 27%

Directions:

1. Softly oil your moderate cooker with cooking oil.

2. Layer half of the hash tans into the base and top with a large portion of the bacon, a large portion of the cheddar, and 33% of the green onions.

3. Put aside some bacon and green onion for, topping and after that rehash with a moment layer of hash cocoa, bacon, cheddar, and onion.

4. In a substantial bowl, whisk together eggs, drain, salt, and pepper and gradually pour over top.

5. Cook until eggs are set, roughly 2-3 hours on high, or 4-5 hours on low.

6. Sprinkle remaining bacon and onions on top and serve promptly, with or without hot sauce.

Hot Chocolate Steel-cut Oatmeal:

Serving Size: 1 cup

Servings per Recipe: 4

Smart Points per Serving: 6

Calories: 126

Cooking Time: Approx. 2 Hours

Ingredients:

- 1 cup steel-cut oats

- 4 cup water

- 1/2 cup coconut milk

- 1 tablespoon cocoa powder

- 1 teaspoon vanilla

- 1/4 teaspoon salt

- 1 tablespoon coconut palm sugar or immaculate maple syrup

- 8 drops fluid stevia

Nutrition Information:

- ✓ Saturated Fat: 6.4 g

- ✓ Cholesterol: 0 mg

- ✓ Sodium: 160 mg

- ✓ Carbohydrates: 12.4 g

- ✓ Dietary Fiber: 2.1 g

- ✓ Sugars: 4.4 g

- ✓ Protein: 2.7 g

Directions:

1. In a substantial bowl, consolidate the water, milk, vanilla, and stevia.

2. Speed in the cocoa, sugar, and salt.

3. At long last, blend in the oats. Oil within your moderate cooker.

4. Pour in the above blend.

5. Set the slow cooker low for 1-2 hours, and swing it to keep warm before resigning to bed.

6. In the morning, put everything a blend and devour!

7. Best with some shaved chocolate in case you're feeling truly degenerated!

Pumpkin Pie Steel-cut Oats:

Serving Size: 1 cup

Servings per Recipe: 4

Smart Points per Serving: 6

Calories: 188

Cooking Time: 8 Hours

Ingredients:

- 1 cup steel cut oats
- 3-1/2 cups water (almond or standard drain can be substituted)
- 1 cup canned pumpkin puree
- 1 teaspoon vanilla concentrate
- 1/4 teaspoon salt
- 1 teaspoon pumpkin pie flavor
- 1/2 cup honey or 2 teaspoons vanilla fluid stevia*
- Sweetener can be included amid cooking

Nutrition Information:

- ✓ Saturated Fat: 0 g
- ✓ Cholesterol: 0 mg
- ✓ Sodium: 193 mg

- ✓ Carbohydrates: 15 g

- ✓ Dietary Fiber: 2 g

- ✓ Sugars: 7 g

- ✓ Protein: 1 g

Directions:

1. Mix all fixings in the slow cooker and cook on low for 8 hours.

2. Server hot

Sausage and Sweet Pepper Hash:

Serving Size: 2-3 cup

Servings per Recipe: 10

Smart Points per Serving: 5

Calories: 131

Cooking Time: Approx. 5 to 6 Hours

Ingredients:

- 12-ounce bundle cooked smoked chicken hot dog with apple, cut into 1/2-inch pieces

- 1 teaspoon olive oil

- 1/2 mugs cut sweet onion

- Nonstick cooking shower

- 1/2 pounds red-cleaned potatoes, cut into 1/2-inch pieces

- 2 teaspoons clipped new thyme or 1/2 teaspoon dried thyme, pounded

- 1/2 teaspoon ground dark pepper

- 1/4 glass lessened sodium chicken soup

- 1/2 glasses slashed green, red, as well as yellow sweet peppers

- 1/2 glass destroyed Swiss cheddar

- 2 teaspoons clipped crisp tarragon or parsley

Nutrition Information:

- ✓ Fat: 3g

- ✓ Cholesterol: 24mg

- ✓ Sodium: 22mg

- ✓ Carbohydrate: 18g

- ✓ Fiber: 2g

- ✓ Sugar: 6g

- ✓ Protein: 7g

Directions:

1. In an expansive nonstick skillet cook wiener over medium warmth around 5 minutes or just until caramelized.

2. Expel from skillet. In a similar skillet warm oil over medium-low warmth.

3. Include onion; cook around 5 minutes or until delicate and simply beginning to cocoa, blending every so often.

4. Coat the base of a 3 1/2-or 4-quart moderate cooker with a cooking shower or line the cooker with a dispensable moderate cooker liner.

5. In the readied cooker consolidate frankfurter, onion, potatoes, thyme, and dark pepper. Pour soup over blend in cooker.

6. Cover and cook on a low warm setting for 5 to 6 hours or on a high warm setting for 2 1/2 to 3 hours.

7. Blend in sweet peppers. In the event that covered, sprinkle with cheddar.

8. In the event that utilizing low warmth setting, swing cooker to high warmth setting.

9. Cover and cook for 15 minutes more. Before serving, sprinkle with tarragon. Utilize an opened spoon for serving.

Banana Pecan French toast:

Serving Size: 2 slice

Servings per Recipe: 6

Smart Points per Serving: 12

Calories: 273

Cooking Time: Approx. 3 to 5 Hours

Ingredients:

- 12 (1" thick) cuts entire wheat baguette
- 4 eggs
- 3/4 glass almond milk
- 1 tablespoon coconut sugar
- 1 tablespoon vanilla
- 1 teaspoon cinnamon
- 2 tablespoons coconut oil, liquefied
- 2 bananas cut
- 1/2 lemons, crispy crushed
- 1/2 cleaved pecans
- Nonstick cooking shower

- Uncontaminated maple syrup for serving

Nutrient Information:

✓ Saturated Fat: 5 g

✓ Sodium: 173 mg

✓ Cholesterol: 124 mg

✓ Carbohydrates: 42 g

✓ Fiber: 2 g

✓ Sugars: 25 g

✓ Protein: 7 g

Directions:

1. Shower a 5-7 quart moderate cooker with a nonstick cooking splash.

2. Organize baguette cuts on the base of the moderate cooker.

3. Whisk together eggs, drain, coconut sugar, vanilla, and cinnamon.

4. Shower over the baguette cuts, making a point to cover each cut totally with the egg blend.

5. In a blending dish, shower banana cuts with new lemon juice, hurling to coat.

6. Put banana cuts on baguettes in the moderate cooker. Shower with softened coconut oil, sprinkle with pecans.

7. Cover and cook on high for 2-3 hours or on low for 4-5 hours, or until cooked through.

8. Cooking times with shift with various cookers so start to check your moderate cooker at the 3-hour stamp and permit to cook just until the bread starts to turn brilliant cocoa around the edges.

9. Shower gently with unadulterated maple syrup to serve.

Crock Pot Almond Rice Pudding:

Serving Size: ¾ cup

Servings per Recipe: 6

Smart Points per Serving: 12

Calories: 366

Cooking Time: Approx. 2 to 4 Hours

Ingredients:

- 2 cups dry long-grain cocoa rice
- 5 cups almond milk
- 1/2 cups raisins
- 3 tablespoons chia seeds, partitioned
- 1 cinnamon stick
- Sweetener if needed

Nutrition Information:

- ✓ Saturated Fat: 2 g
- ✓ Cholesterol: 15 mg
- ✓ Sodium: 51 mg
- ✓ Carbohydrates: 69 g
- ✓ Dietary Fiber: 1 g
- ✓ Sugars: 10 g
- ✓ Protein: 12 g

Directions:

1. Include the rice, almond milk, raisins, 2 tablespoons of chia seeds and cinnamon stick in the moderate cooker.

2. Cover and cook on low 3 to 4 hours or high for 1-1/2 to 2 hours, or until rice is delicate.

3. On the off chance that utilizing unsweetened almond milk, include either 1/2 cups of coconut sugar, maple syrup or honey before expelling from the moderate cooker.

4. Sprinkle the rest of the chia seeds before serving.

Blueberry Nutty Banana Oatmeal:

Serving Size: 1 cup

Servings per Recipe: 6

Smart Points per Serving: 13

Calories: 346

Cooking Time: Approx. 2 to 4 Hours

Ingredients:

- 2 cups of rolled oats
- 1/4 cup of toasted almonds
- 1/4 cup of chopped pecans
- 1/4 cup of chopped walnuts
- 2 cups milk
- 1 egg
- 2 bananas, sliced
- 1 cup fresh blueberries
- 1 teaspoon of ground ginger
- 2 tablespoons of ground flax seed

- 1 teaspoon of cinnamon

- 1/4 teaspoon of salt for taste

- 1/2 tablespoon of baking powder

- 2 tablespoons of coconut sugar

- 1 tablespoon pure maple syrup

- 1 teaspoon pure vanilla extract

- 1 tablespoon butter, melted

- Vanilla yogurt for serving

Nutrition Information:

- ✓ Saturated Fat: 4 g

- ✓ Cholesterol: 39 mg

- ✓ Sodium: 145 mg

- ✓ Carbohydrates: 45 g

- ✓ Dietary Fiber: 7 g

- ✓ Sugars: 17g

- ✓ Protein: 11 g

Directions:

1. Join the oats, nuts, flax, flavors, heating powder, and coconut sugar in an expansive bowl.

2. Blend until joined. In a different bowl, beat the milk, egg, maple syrup and vanilla concentrate.

3. Layer the bananas and blueberries in your moderate cooker pot. Spread equally with the oats.

4. Pour the milk blend over top and sprinkle with the margarine.

5. Cook on low warmth for 2-4 hours, until fluid is ingested and the top is gently caramelized.

6. Serve warm, finished with the yogurt if preferred.

Delicious Potato Oatmeal:

Serving Size: 1 cup

Servings per Recipe: 6

Smart Points per Serving: 6

Calories: 164

Cooking Time: Approx. 2 Hours

Ingredients:

- 1 cup of steel cut oats

- 2 cups of low-fat drain

- 2 cups of water

- 1 cup ground sweet potato or 1/2 glass cooked and crushed sweet potato

- 2 tablespoons organic sweetener, pretty much to taste

- Honey or 100% unadulterated maple syrup for taste

- Kosher or Sea salt to taste

- 1/2 teaspoon cinnamon

- 1 teaspoon pumpkin pie flavor

Nutrition Information:

- ✓ Saturated Fats: 1g

- ✓ Cholesterol: 3 mg

- ✓ Sodium: 56 mg

- ✓ Carbohydrates: 45 g

- ✓ Dietary Fiber: 5 g

- ✓ Sugars: 14 g

- ✓ Protein: 8 g

Directions:

1. Combine all ingredients in the cooker, wrap and cook on a low temperature for approximately 2 hours, or until desired uniformity is reached.

2. Recommend 4-5 quart slow cooker.

3. If desired, add chopped raisins and nuts.

1.

Lunch Recipes

Delicious Slow Cook Beef Stew:

Serving Size: 1 cup

Servings per Recipe: 8

Smart Points per Serving: 8

Calories: 274

Cooking Time: 8 Hours

Ingredients:

- 2 tablespoons olive oil

- 1 pound lean hamburger stew meat, cubed in around 1-inch pieces

- 2 tablespoons flour for covering the hamburger

- 1 cup red wine, (discretionary non-alcoholic wine or vegetable juices)

- 5 red potatoes, cubed

- 1 white onion, diced

- 1 cup carrots, sliced/cubed

- 1 cup celery, sliced/cubed

- 1/2 cup mushrooms cut

- 1 cup peas, frozen or fresh

- 4 garlic cloves, minced

- 1/4 cup tomato puree

- 1 tablespoon soy sauce

- 2 tablespoons horseradish

- 2 cups low sodium hamburger juices

- 3 tablespoons balsamic vinegar

- 2 narrows bay leaves

- 2 sprigs fresh thymes

- 1 teaspoon dried parsley

- 1 teaspoon dried oregano

- 1 teaspoon black pepper

- 1/2 teaspoon sea salt

Nutrition Information:

- ✓ Saturated Fat: 2g
- ✓ Cholesterol: 37mg
- ✓ Sodium: 532mg
- ✓ Carbohydrates: 37g
- ✓ Fiber: 5g
- ✓ Sugar: 7g
- ✓ Protein: 19g

Directions:

1. Start by heating oil in a skillet over medium-high temperature.
2. Toss the meat in the flour then add to the cooker.
3. Make them brown on all sides for around two minutes—meat doesn't need to be cooked through, simply get a pleasant covering on it!
4. Add wine and blend it to relax the bits off the base of the dish.
5. Bring down warmth to medium and stew for 5 minutes.
6. Include the meat, container sauce, and all the rest of the ingredients to the slow cooker.
7. Cover and cook on low for 7 to 8 hours, or high for 4 to 5 hours.
8. Expel the inlet leaves and thyme, and serve!

Amazing Thai Chicken Soup:

Serving Size: 1 cup

Servings per Recipe: 8

Smart Points per Serving: 11

Calories: 269

Cooking Time: 4 to 8 Hours

Ingredients:

- 5 chicken thighs, skinless and boneless
- 6 cups chicken stock, no fat
- 1 (14.5 ounces) can coconut milk (full-fat)
- 1 teaspoon kosher salt
- 1/2 teaspoon black pepper
- 4 teaspoons ground ginger
- 1 teaspoon red curry powder
- 1 (4.5 ounces) can diced jalapeños
- 1 red bell pepper, seeded and diced
- 1 onion, diced
- 3 carrots, sliced
- 1 big potato, cut into little shapes
- Juice of 1 lime
- 1/4 cup crisply chopped cilantro

Nutrition Information:

- ✓ Saturated Fat: 11g

- ✓ Cholesterol: 25mg

- ✓ Sodium: 812mg

- ✓ Carbohydrates: 24g

- ✓ Fiber: 4g

- ✓ Sugar: 6g

- ✓ Protein: 14g

Directions:

1. Include all ingredients, aside from cilantro, to the slow cooker.

2. Cover and cook on low 6 to 8 hours or high 3 to 4 hours.

3. At the point when carrots are delicate and chicken is done, expel chicken and shred with a fork.

4. Return destroyed chicken and a large portion of the cilantro to the soup.

5. Mix soup and serve!

Slow Cook Bourbon Chicken:

Serving Size: 1 cup

Servings per Recipe: 5

Smart Points per Serving: 8

Calories: 380

Cooking Time: 4 to 8 Hours

Ingredients:

- 3 tablespoons molasses or nectar
- 1/4 cup ketchup
- 3 tablespoons apple juice vinegar
- 1/4 cup water
- 5 boneless skinless chicken breasts
- 1/2 teaspoon ground ginger
- 4 cloves garlic, minced
- 1/4 teaspoon pounded red stew drops
- 1/4 cup sans sugar squeezed apple
- 1/4 cup (great quality) Bourbon
- 1/4 cup low-sodium soy sauce
- 1 teaspoon Kosher or sea salt
- 1/2 teaspoon black pepper
- 1/4 cup cut green onions, decorate

Nutrition Information:

- ✓ Saturated Fat: 1g
- ✓ Cholesterol: 172mg
- ✓ Sodium: 745mg
- ✓ Carbohydrates: 17g
- ✓ Fiber: 0g

✓ Sugar: 14g

✓ Protein: 32g

Directions:

1. Put chicken breasts into a moderate cooker.

2. Whisk together all the rest of the ingredients in a bowl then pour over chicken.

3. Cook on low 4-5 hours or high for 2-3 hours.

4. When cooking is finished, evacuate chicken and shred it.

5. Return chicken to moderate cooker and cook on low for an additional 15 minutes.

6. On the off chance that coveted, serve over cocoa rice with green onions on top.

Protein Chicken Tacos:

Serving Size: 1

Servings per Recipe: 8

Smart Points per Serving: 11

Calories: 382

Cooking Time: 4 to 8 Hours

Ingredients:

- 1 pound boneless skinless chicken breast

- 3 cups no sugar included salsa

- 1 teaspoon ground cumin

- 2 tablespoons stew powder

- 1/2 cup corn kernels

- 1/2 cup black beans

- 1/2 cup low sodium chicken soup

- 8 entire wheat flour tortillas

- 1 cup destroyed Romaine lettuce

- 1 huge tomato, diced

- 1 cup low-fat grated cheddar

- 1/4 cup diced avocado

- 1/4 cup plain Greek yogurt

Nutrition Information:

- ✓ Saturated Fat: 4g

- ✓ Cholesterol: 57mg

- ✓ Sodium: 1237mg

- ✓ Carbohydrates: 44g

- ✓ Fiber: 6g

- ✓ Sugar: 7g

- ✓ Protein: 26g

Directions:

1. In a slow cooker, include chicken, salsa, cumin, black beans, chili powder, corn, and juices.

2. Cook on low for 8 hours or high for 4 hours.

3. Remove delicate chicken from cooker and shred with a fork.

4. Come back to a moderate cooker and cook for an additional 30 minutes on low or 15 minutes on high.

5. Spoon around 2 tablespoons of destroyed chicken into every tortilla.

6. Beat with lettuce, tomato, cheddar, avocado, and yogurt.

7. Serve and appreciate!

Chicken with Lemon and Garlic

Serving Size: 1

Servings per Recipe: 6

Smart Points per Serving: 3

Calories: 167

Cooking Time: 6 Hours

Ingredients:

- Ground black pepper (to taste)

- Sea salt (to taste)

- Thyme (1 T dried)

- Chicken broth (1 cup)

- Lemons (3 sliced)

- Garlic (10 cloves chopped)

- Chicken breasts (6 fillets, 2 lbs.)

Nutrition Information:

- ✓ Protein: 30 grams
- ✓ Carbs: 36 grams
- ✓ Fats: 2 grams
- ✓ Saturated Fats: 1.5 grams
- ✓ Sugar: 0 grams
- ✓ Fiber 0 grams
- ✓ Calories: 167

Directions:

1. Prepare the slow cooker by spraying the bottom using a cooking spray to ensure nothing sticks. Place 5 cloves of garlic and 1.5 lemons directly on the bottom.

2. Season the chicken as desired before setting it atop the garlic and lemons. Top the chicken with the remaining garlic and lemons before adding in the chicken broth. Cover the slow cooker and let it cook on a low setting for 6 hours.

3. Strain the liquid in the slower cooker and use it to top the chicken prior to serving.

<u>Chicken and Rice Casserole:</u>

Serving Size: 1 cup

Servings per Recipe: 4

Smart Points per Serving: 9

Calories: 327

Cooking Time: 8 Hours

Ingredients:

- 4 (about 1.5 p.) new boneless, skinless chicken thighs or bosoms, cut into pieces of around 1-inch
- 1 tablespoon additional virgin olive oil
- 3 cups chicken stock, no fat
- 2 vast carrots, peeled and cut into 1/2-inch rounds
- 1/2 teaspoon fit or sea salt, pretty much to taste
- 1/4 teaspoon dark pepper
- 2 cups cooked cocoa rice or quinoa
- 1 cup (defrosted) peas
- 1/2 cup ground parmesan cheddar

Nutrition Information:

- ✓ Saturated Fat: 3 g
- ✓ Sodium: 833 mg
- ✓ Cholesterol: 78 mg
- ✓ Carbohydrates: 36 g
- ✓ Fiber: 3 g
- ✓ Sugars: 6 g
- ✓ Protein: 25 g

Directions:

1. In the slow cooker, include the chicken, olive oil, carrots, juices, salt, and pepper.

2. Cover up and cook on low temperature for 6 to 8 hours or on high flame for 3 to 4, or until chicken is done and carrots delicate.

3. Whenever cooked, include pre-cooked rice, peas, and parmesan.

4. Blend to join and keep cooking for 10 minutes.

Honey Mustard Chicken:

Serving Size: 1 cup

Servings per Recipe: 4

Smart Points per Serving: 9

Calories: 327

Cooking Time: 8 Hours

Ingredients:

- 4 (1.5 pounds) new boneless, skinless chicken thighs or breasts, cut into chunks of around 1-inch

- 1 tablespoon extra-virgin olive oil

- 3 cups chicken stock, no fat

- 2 substantial carrots, peeled and cut into 1/2-inch rounds

- 1/2 teaspoon genuine or ocean salt, pretty much to taste

- 1/4 teaspoon black pepper

- 2 cups cooked brown rice or quinoa

- 1 cup (defrosted) peas

- 1/2 cup ground parmesan cheddar

Nutrition Information:

- ✓ Saturated Fat: 2 g

- ✓ Sodium: 525 mg

- ✓ Cholesterol: 66 mg

- ✓ Carbohydrates: 19 g

- ✓ Fiber: 1 g

- ✓ Sugars: 17 g

- ✓ Protein: 14 g

Directions:

1. In the cooker, include the chicken, olive oil, carrots, stock, salt, and pepper.

2. Cover up and cook on low temperature for 6 to 8 hours or on high flame for 3 to 4, or until chicken is done and carrots delicate.

3. Whenever cooked, include pre-cooked rice, peas, and parmesan.

4. Blend to join and keep cooking for 10 minutes.

Slow Cook Chicken Cheese Steak

Serving Size: 1

Servings per Recipe: 5

Smart Points per Serving: 7

Calories: 313

Cooking Time: 6 Hours

Ingredients:

- Ground black pepper (to taste)
- Sea salt (to taste)
- Rolls (6)
- Steak seasoning (2 T)
- Garlic cloves (2 chopped)
- Provolone cheese (6 slices)
- Green peppers (2 sliced thin)
- Onion (1 sliced)
- Light butter (2 T)
- Chicken breasts (1 lb.)

Nutrition Information:

- ✓ Protein: 29 grams
- ✓ Carbs: 28 grams
- ✓ Fats: 6.5 grams
- ✓ Saturated Fats: 1.5 grams
- ✓ Sugar: 1 grams
- ✓ Fiber 2.5 grams
- ✓ Calories: 313

Directions:

1. Thinly slice the chicken into strips before adding it to a bowl and seasoning with steak seasoning, pepper and salt as needed.

2. Add the butter to the slow cooker before adding in the green peppers as well as the onions and then top it all with the chick.

3. Cover the slow cooker and let it cook on a low heat for 5 hours.

4. Divide the results into 6 servings and add the results to each roll before topping with the cheese and toasting for 2 minutes prior to serving.

Taco Bowl with Slow Cooker Chicken and Salsa

Serving Size: 1

Servings per Recipe: 6

Smart Points per Serving: 9

Calories: 391

Cooking Time: 6 Hours

Ingredients:

- Ground black pepper (to taste)

- Sea salt (to taste)

- Lime juice (1 lime)

- Tomatoes (2 diced fine)

- Red onion (1 diced)

- Avocado (1 sliced into 12 pieces)

- Brown rice (1 cup cooked)

- Cilantro (.5 cups chopped)

- Low fat sour cream (.75 cups)

- Shred Mexican cheese blend (6 oz.)

- Black beans (15 oz. rinsed, drained)

- Salsa (16 oz.)

- Chicken breast (1 lb. boneless, skinless)

Nutrition Information:

- ✓ Protein: 29 grams

- ✓ Carbs: 40 grams

- ✓ Fats: 12 grams

- ✓ Saturated Fats: 3.4 grams

- ✓ Sugar: 1.2 grams

- ✓ Fiber 7.5 grams

- ✓ Calories: 391

Directions:

1. Add the chicken as well as the salsa to the slow cooker and let them cook, covered, on a low setting for 6 hours.

2. Combine the pepper, salt, lime juice, onions and tomatoes together in a small bowl.

3. Create each taco as desired before topping with the mixture from the bowl, 2 slices of avocado, cilantro and 2 T sour cream. Serve promptly for best results.

Sweet and Sour Chicken

Serving Size: 1

Servings per Recipe: 6

Smart Points per Serving: 6

Calories: 241

Cooking Time: 6 Hours

Ingredients:

- Ground black pepper (to taste)

- Sea salt (to taste)

- Corn starch (2 T)

- Garlic (6 cloves minced)

- Soy sauce (.25 cups)

- Lemon lime soda (.25 cups)

- White vinegar (.5 cups)

- Brown sugar (.5 cups)

- Chicken breast (6 fillets, 2 lbs.)

Nutrition Information:

- ✓ Protein: 21 grams
- ✓ Carbs: 20 grams
- ✓ Fats: 2 grams
- ✓ Saturated Fats: .5 grams
- ✓ Sugar: 0 grams
- ✓ Fiber 0 grams
- ✓ Calories: 241

Directions:

1. Season the chicken as desired before adding it into the slow cooker.

2. Combine the rest of the ingredients aside from the cornstarch and add it in on top of the chicken.

3. Cover the slow cooker and let it cook on a low heat for 6 hours.

4. Take the chicken out of the slow cooker and set it aside before pouring what's left into a sauce pan and then placing it on the stove on top of a burner set to a high heat.

5. As it is heating, mix the cornstarch together with a small amount of water before adding that to the saucepan. Let the pan simmer and stir thoroughly to ensure it thickens. Do this for three minutes and then let is rest for 1 additional minute.

6. Top chicken with sauce prior to serving.

Slow Cook Balsamic Chicken

Serving Size: 1

Servings per Recipe: 4

Smart Points per Serving: 4

Calories: 191

Cooking Time: 6 Hours

Ingredients:

- Ground black pepper (to taste)
- Sea salt (to taste)
- Balsamic vinegar (.5 cups)
- Portabella mushrooms (10 oz. sliced thick)
- Pears (2 sliced, cored)
- Chicken breast (1 lb.)

Nutrition Information:

- ✓ Protein: 25 grams
- ✓ Carbs: 15 grams
- ✓ Fats: 1.5 grams
- ✓ Saturated Fats: 2.4 grams
- ✓ Sugar: 2 grams
- ✓ Fiber 3 grams
- ✓ Calories: 191

Directions:

1. Add all of the ingredients to a slow cooker and let them cook, covered, on a low setting for 6 hours.

Bean and Potato Soup:

Serving Size: 1 1/2 cup

Servings per Recipe: 8 cup

Smart Points per Serving: 8

Calories: 287

Cooking Time: 8 Hours

Ingredients:

- 1 pound Yukon gold potatoes, peeled and slashed (around 3-4 cups crushed)

- 2 jars northern beans, drained and cleansed

- 1/2 cup slashed onions or shallots

- 2 garlic cloves, minced

- 1/2 cup slashed carrots

- 1/2 cup slashed celery

- 2 tablespoons finely slashed new rosemary or 2 teaspoons dried rosemary

- 1/2 tablespoon finely slashed new oregano or 1 teaspoon dried oregano

- 2 tablespoons crisp thyme leaves or 2 teaspoons dried thyme

- 1 teaspoon fit or ocean salt

- 1/4 teaspoon dark pepper

- 1 teaspoon pounded red pepper chips, discretionary, pretty much for heat fancied

- 4 cups low-sodium vegetable or chicken stock

- 1 parmesan skin or 1 (2-inch) piece parmesan, optional*

- 1 tablespoon additional virgin olive oil

- 1 bay leaf

Nutrition Information:

- ✓ Saturated Fat: 1g

- ✓ Cholesterol: 2mg

- ✓ Sodium: 91mg

- ✓ Carbohydrates: 53g

- ✓ Fiber: 10g

- ✓ Sugars: 2g

- ✓ Protein: 13g

Directions:

1. Add all fixings to the simmering pot and mix.

2. Allow to cook on low for 6-8 hours or high for 5 hours.

3. Remove including the parmesan skin or a bit of parmesan includes a considerable measure of appetizing flavor to the soup and serve.

White Bean and Chicken Chili:

Serving Size: 1 cup

Servings per Recipe: 12 cup

Smart Points per Serving: 8

Calories: 315

Cooking Time: 8 Hours

Ingredients:

- 2 pounds boneless, skinless chicken breasts, cut into bite on pieces (around 1/2-inch)

- 1 little sweet onion, diced

- 2 cloves garlic, minced

- 2 jalapeño peppers, seeded and diced

- 1 medium Poblano pepper, seeded and diced

- 2 (4 ounces) jars diced green chilies

- 1 teaspoon legitimate or ocean salt, pretty much to taste

- 1 tablespoon stew powder

- 2 teaspoons cumin

- 1/2 teaspoon black pepper

- 1 teaspoon dried oregano

- 1/4 cup newly cleaved cilantro

- 3 (15-ounce) jars cannellini beans

- 4 cups chicken soup, sans fat, low-sodium

- 1/2 cup decreased fat ground cheddar

- 1 cup low-fat sour cream or Greek yogurt

Nutrition Information:

- ✓ Saturated Fat: 3g

- ✓ Cholesterol: 69mg

- ✓ Sodium: 223mg

- ✓ Carbohydrates: 31g

- ✓ Fiber: 6g

- ✓ Sugars: 4g

- ✓ Protein: 30g

Directions:

1. Include all ingredients, with the exception of cheddar and yogurt, to the moderate cooker, mixed well.

2. Wrap and cook on low temperature for 6-8 hours or high temperature for 3-4 hours.

3. The most recent 30 minutes of cooking time, include the harsh cream and cheddar, blend to consolidate.

4. Cover and keep cooking 30 minutes.

5. On the off chance that covered, before serving orderly with sour cream, cheddar, and cilantro.

Slow Cook Chicken Teriyaki

Serving Size: 1

Servings per Recipe: 4

Smart Points per Serving: 5

Calories: 217

Cooking Time: 6 Hours

Ingredients:

- Ground black pepper (to taste)

- Brown sugar (.25 cups)

- Soy sauce (.5 cups)

- Yellow pepper (.5 sliced thin)

- Red bell pepper (.5 sliced thin)

- Garlic (2 cloves minced)

- Pineapple (16 oz. chopped)

- Chicken breast (1 lb. cubed)

Nutrition Information:

- ✓ Protein: 27 grams

- ✓ Carbs: 25 grams

- ✓ Fats: 2 grams

- ✓ Saturated Fats: 1 gram

- ✓ Sugar: 1.7 grams

- ✓ Fiber 7 grams

- ✓ Calories: 217

Directions:

1. In a small bowl, combine the brown sugar, black pepper, garlic and soy sauce and mix well.

2. Add the chicken to the slow cooker before topping with the soy sauce mixture and the pineapple.

3. Cover the slow cooker and let it cook on a low setting for 6 hours, after 5 hours remove the lid to allow the sauce to thicken.

One Pot Chicken Curry

Serving Size: 1

Servings per Recipe: 4

Smart Points per Serving: 6

Calories: 272

Cooking Time: 4 Hours

Ingredients:

- Ground black pepper (to taste)
- Sea salt (to taste)
- Cornstarch (1 T)
- Brown sugar (2 T)
- Curry paste (3 T)
- Lime juice (1 lime)
- Garlic cloves (5 minced)
- Coconut milk (15 oz.)
- Stir fry vegetables (16 oz.)
- Yellow onion (1 sliced thin)
- Chicken breast (1 lb. diced)

Nutrition Information:

- ✓ Protein: 28 grams
- ✓ Carbs: 17 grams
- ✓ Fats: 9 grams

- ✓ Saturated Fats: 2.7 grams
- ✓ Sugar: 9 grams
- ✓ Fiber 3 grams
- ✓ Calories: 272

Directions:

1. Season chicken as desired before adding it to the slow cooker and covering it with the onion.

2. Combine the curry paste, sugar, garlic, lime juice and coconut milk in a bowl and mix well.

3. Add the results to the slow cooker and cook, covered, on a low setting for 5 hours.

4. When there is half an hour of cooking time remaining, mix in the vegetables as well as the cornstarch mixed with 1 T water.

Yummy Chicken Italiano

Serving Size: 1

Servings per Recipe: 6

Smart Points per Serving: 5

Calories: 225

Cooking Time: 6 Hours

Ingredients:

- Ground black pepper (to taste)

- Sea salt (to taste)

- Paprika (2 tsp.)

- Chicken broth (1 cup)

- White wine (1 cup)

- Light butter (1 T)

- Cream cheese (8 oz.)

- Italian dressing mix (1 packet)

- Portabella mushrooms (8 oz. sliced)

- Mushrooms (8 oz. sliced)

- Chicken breast (1.5 lbs.)

Nutrition Information:

- ✓ Protein: 31 grams

- ✓ Carbs: 9 grams

- ✓ Fats: 3 grams

- ✓ Saturated Fats: 5.7 grams

- ✓ Sugar: 3 grams

- ✓ Fiber 1 grams

- ✓ Calories: 225

What to Use

Directions:

1. Add the butter to a saucepan before placing it on the stove on top of a burner set to a medium heat and mix in the Italian dressing thoroughly.

2. Add in the chicken broth, wine and cream cheese and keep stirring until the cream cheese has melted.

3. Add the mushrooms to the slow cooker before seasoning the chicken and adding it in as well.

4. Add all of the ingredients to a slow cooker and let them cook, covered, on a low setting for 6 hours.

Delicious Sweet Potato Chili:

Serving Size: 1 cup

Servings per Recipe: 6 cup

Smart Points per Serving: 8

Calories: 275

Cooking Time: 6 to 8 Hours

Ingredients:

- 1 pound ground turkey

- 1 sweet onion, diced

- 1 jalapeno, seeded and minced

- 3 garlic cloves, minced

- 2 sweet potatoes, cubed

- 1 (14.5 ounces) can dark beans

- 1 (14.5 ounces) fire simmered pulverized tomatoes

- 2 cups low-sodium chicken juices

- 1 teaspoon cinnamon

- 1 tablespoon bean stew powder

- 1 teaspoon cumin

- 1 teaspoon sea salt

- 1/2 teaspoon dark pepper

- 1 tablespoon unsweetened cocoa powder

Nutrition Information:

- ✓ Saturated Fat: 2g

- ✓ Cholesterol: 52mg

- ✓ Sodium: 676mg

- ✓ Carbohydrates: 33g

- ✓ Fiber: 9g

- ✓ Sugar: 8g

- ✓ Protein: 23g

Directions:

1. Add all ingredients to the slow cooker, separating the ground turkey into bits with a wood spoon.

2. Blend to consolidate. Boil on low flame for 6 to 8 hours or high flame for 3 to 4 hours.

3. On the off chance that coveted, present with a dab of sour cream or Greek yogurt and entire grain tortillas disintegrated on top.

Slow Cook Pumpkin Chili:

Serving Size: 1 cup

Servings per Recipe: 6 cup

Smart Points per Serving: 7

Calories: 214

Cooking Time: 6 to 8 Hours

Ingredients:

- 1 onion, diced

- 2 (14 ounce) cans crushed tomatoes

- 2 (14 ounces) cans black beans, a drained

- 1 carrot, shredded

- 1 bell pepper, diced

- 1 jalapeno, veins and seeds removed and minced

- 2 cloves garlic, minced

- 1 1/2 cups pumpkin puree

- 1 cups low sodium vegetable broth

- 2 tablespoons chili powder

- 1 teaspoon pumpkin pie spice

- 1 teaspoon kosher salt

- 1/2 teaspoon black pepper

Nutrition Information:

- ✓ Saturated Fat: 0g

- ✓ Cholesterol: 0mg

- ✓ Sodium: 841mg

- ✓ Carbohydrates: 43g

- ✓ Fiber: 16g

- ✓ Sugar: 11g

- ✓ Protein: 12g

Directions:

1. Add everything to your slow cooker and stir to combine.

2. Cook on low for 5 to 6 hours or high for 2 to 3 hours.

3. Present with a spoonful of Greek yogurt or avocado slices.

Apple Butter Pulled Pork:

Serving Size: 1 cup

Servings per Recipe: 6 cup

Smart Points per Serving: 12

Calories: 352

Cooking Time: 2 Hours

Ingredients:

- 5 apples, peeled, cored and diced
- 2 teaspoons cinnamon
- 1/2 teaspoon nutmeg
- 1/4 teaspoon allspice
- 1/4 teaspoon ground cloves
- 1/4 cup coconut sugar
- 1/4 cup apple cider vinegar
- 3 cloves of garlic, minced
- 1 medium onion, chopped
- 1 tablespoon spicy brown mustard
- 1 teaspoon kosher salt
- 1/2 teaspoon black pepper
- 4 pork loin chops

Nutrition Information:

- ✓ Saturated Fat: 4g
- ✓ Cholesterol: 92mg
- ✓ Sodium: 426mg
- ✓ Carbohydrates: 33g
- ✓ Fiber: 5g

✓ Sugar: 23g

✓ Protein: 28g

Directions:

1. Place apples, cinnamon, nutmeg, allspice and coconut sugar into slow cooker.

2. Cook on low for four hours, or high for two hours.

3. Add cider vinegar, garlic, onion, mustard, salt, and pepper.

4. Combine the apples, then adjoin pork chops.

5. Wrap the chops with the apple mix. Cook for an additional four hours on low down temperature, or maximum two hours on high flame.

6. Remove pork, shred and return to the slow cooker.

7. Roast on high flame for ten more minutes or so, and then serve!

Loaded Creamy Corn Chowder:

Serving Size: 1 ½ cup

Servings per Recipe: 6

Smart Points per Serving: 9

Calories: 269

Cooking Time: Approx. 4 to 8 Hours

Ingredients:

FOR THE CHOWDER:

- 4 cups vegetable stock
- 2 cups almond milk, unsweetened or 2 cups canned coconut milk (creamier outcomes)
- 2 1/2 tablespoons cornstarch
- 2 tablespoons olive oil
- 1 teaspoon garlic powder
- 1 teaspoon onion powder
- 3/4 teaspoon salt
- 1/2 teaspoon pepper
- 2 cups red potato, diced
- 1 (16-ounce) bundle solidified corn

FOR THE TOPPINGS:

- 1/4 cup diced tomato
- 1/4 cup diced purple onion
- 1/4 cup daintily cut scallions
- 1/4 cup decreased fat cheddar

Nutrition Information:

- ✓ Saturated Fat: 4 g
- ✓ Cholesterol: 14 mg
- ✓ Sodium: 152 mg
- ✓ Carbohydrates: 34 g
- ✓ Dietary Fiber: 3 g
- ✓ Sugars: 8 g
- ✓ Protein: 10 g

Directions:

1. In a 3-4 quart moderate cooker, whisk together vegetable stock, almond milk, cornstarch, olive oil, garlic powder, onion powder, salt, and pepper.

2. Mix in potato and corn. Cover up and cook on low temperature for 6 to 7 hours or on high flame for 3 to 4 hours.

3. Serve finished with your most loved fixings.

4. For creamier result, expel 2-3 cups of the chowder before serving and add them to a blender.

5. Puree on high and after that arrival to the soup, blending.

6. On the other hand, you can embed a hand blender into the soup and puree until covered surface/level of richness is accomplished.

Chunky Squash and Chicken Stew:

Serving Size: 2 cup

Servings per Recipe: 4

Smart Points per Serving: 8

Calories: 297

Cooking Time: Approx. 4 Hours

Ingredients:

*   15 ounces chicken bosoms, hacked into nibble estimated pieces
*   Flour, for covering

- 1/2 teaspoon salt

- 1/8 teaspoon pepper

- 2 tablespoons additional virgin olive oil

- 2 1/2 cups chicken juices

- 1 medium onion, coarsely slashed

- 14 ounces squash, diced

- 1-1/2 cups vegetable juices

- 3 crisp sage leaves, chopped or torn

Nutrition Information:

- ✓ Saturated Fat: 2 g

- ✓ Cholesterol: 69 mg

- ✓ Sodium: 245 mg

- ✓ Carbohydrates: 21 g

- ✓ Sugars: 5 g

- ✓ Protein: 27 g

Directions:

1. Coat the chicken with flour and shake off the abundance.

2. Over medium warmth, in a pan with additional virgin olive oil, chestnut the chicken then season with salt and pepper.

3. Try not to stuff. Cook in clusters if necessary. Pour 1 cup chicken soup in the pan and cook until the sauce thickens.

4. Exchange the substance of the pan to the moderate cooker. Include a smidgen all the more additional virgin olive oil in the pot then sauté the onions over low - medium warmth for around 5 minutes.

5. Exchange the onions to the moderate cooker. Include the squash, staying chicken stock, and sage in the moderate cooker.

6. Set on low for 4 hours.

Slow Cook Tasty Beef:

Serving Size: 1/10

Servings per Recipe: 10

Smart Points per Serving: 13

Calories: 400

Cooking Time: Approx. 8 Hours

Ingredients:

- 1 (3-pound) meat (round or chuck)
- 1/4 cup additional virgin olive oil
- 1/4 cup crushed garlic
- 1/2 teaspoons ocean salt
- 1 teaspoon pepper
- 1/2 cup veggie or meat soup

Nutrition Information:

- ✓ Saturated Fat: 11 g
- ✓ Cholesterol: 124 mg

- ✓ Sodium: 229 mg

- ✓ Carbohydrates: 2 g

- ✓ Sugars: 0 g

- ✓ Protein: 27 g

Directions:

1. Put meat in a 4-quart cooker. Sprinkle with olive oil, garlic, sea salt, and pepper.

2. Pour veggie soup around the outside of the meat.

3. Cover and cook on low for 8-10 hours or on high for 6-8 hours.

4. At the point when the meat is amazingly delicate, expel it from the slow cooker and shred with a fork.

5. Serve in tacos, with your most loved sauce and pureed potatoes, mix it into bean stew, cook it into Shepherd's Pie, or top it with teriyaki sauce.

6. Serve it over cocoa rice.

Cauliflower Fried Rice:

Serving Size: 2 cups

Servings per Recipe: 4

Smart Points per Serving: 5

Calories: 172

Cooking Time: Approx. 4 to 8 Hours

Ingredients:

- 2 heads cauliflower

- 2 tablespoons ginger-garlic puree (or new garlic and ginger root, peeled and minced)

- 1/2 cup vegetable soup

- 2 eggs

- 1 cup solidified vegetable blend

- 1/2 cup Boars Head turkey ham, diced (discretionary)

- 1/4 cup green onions, diced

- 1/4 cup cilantro (discretionary)

- 2 tablespoons lite (low-sodium) soy sauce or to taste

Nutrition Information:

- ✓ Saturated Fat: 2 g

- ✓ Cholesterol: 92 mg

- ✓ Sodium: 405 mg

- ✓ Carbohydrates: 22 g

- ✓ Sugars: 6 g

- ✓ Protein: 13 g

Directions:

1. Cut the florets off each head of cauliflower.

2. Put the florets in an extensive nourishment processor.

3. Beat until finely disintegrated.

4. In an extensive simmering pot, include cauliflower pieces, ginger garlic puree, and vegetable stock.

5. Cover and cook on high for 2 hours or on low for 3-4 hours.

6. 30 minutes prior to plating, beat the eggs together and mix them in a saucepan.

7. Include eggs, solidified veggies, and diced turkey ham (if craved) to the simmering pot.

8. Permit to cook for 30 minutes more, or until the solidified veggies are warm.

9. Mix in green onions and cilantro. Soy sauce to taste.

10. Serve and enjoy!

Dinner Recipes

Buffalo Turkey Meatballs:

Serving Size: 3

Servings per Recipe: 18

Smart Points per Serving: 10

Calories: 274

Cooking Time: Approx. 4 Hours

Ingredients:

For Meatballs

- 1/4 cup non-fat milk
- 2 cuts entire wheat sandwich bread
- 14 ounces lean, ground chicken or turkey
- 1 teaspoon salt, partitioned
- 1/4 teaspoon pepper
- 1/4 teaspoon cayenne pepper
- 1/2 cup Parmesan cheddar
- 1 egg

For Sauce

- 2 teaspoons olive oil
- 1 little sweet onions, diced
- 2 cloves garlic, minced
- 1 cup hot sauce
- 1 (4 ounces) can dice green chilies
- 1/2 cup nectar
- 1 teaspoon bean stew powder
- 1 teaspoon paprika

- 1/4 teaspoon cayenne pepper

- 1/2 teaspoon dark pepper

- 1 teaspoon genuine or ocean salt

Nutrition Information:

- ✓ Saturated Fat: 4g

- ✓ Cholesterol: 91mg

- ✓ Sodium: 1630mg

- ✓ Carbohydrates: 27g

- ✓ Sugar: 19g

- ✓ Protein: 18g

Directions:

1. Preheat stove to 450 degrees and line a preparing sheet with aluminum thwart.

2. In a little bowl, absorb the bread the milk. In an extensive bowl, blend the chicken or turkey, Parmesan, 1/2 teaspoon salt, pepper, egg, and the bread absorbed milk.

3. Blend well until it gets to be distinctly conservative.

4. Get about a tablespoon of the meat then come in the middle of your palms to make the meatballs—we made them utilizing a 1" scoop.

5. Put them on the heating sheet. Cook for 6 minutes.

6. For the sauce, warm the olive oil on medium-low. Include the onions and garlic and sauté until onions are translucent.

7. Include the onions, garlic, and every one of extra fixings to a bowl and race until smooth.

8. Add enough meatballs to cover the base of the moderate cooker, and then pour half of the sauce.

9. Include the rest of the meatballs and pour whatever remains of the sauce.

10. Cover and cook on low 2-4 hours, or until meatballs are cooked through.

Slow Cooker Beef and Barbeque

Serving Size: 2

Servings per Recipe: 8

Smart Points per Serving: 9

Calories: 313

Cooking Time: Approx. 6 Hours

Ingredients:

- Ground black pepper (to taste)
- Sea salt (to taste)
- Cayenne pepper (.25 tsp.)
- Paprika (1 tsp.)
- Garlic powder (1 tsp.)
- Onion powder (1 T)
- Worcestershire sauce (2 tsp.)
- Hot sauce (1 T)
- Brown sugar (.5 cups)
- Yellow mustard (.5 cups)
- Ketchup (1 cup)
- Apple cider vinegar (1 cup)
- Beef roast (2 lbs.)

Nutrition Information:

- ✓ Protein: 25 grams
- ✓ Carbs: 17 grams
- ✓ Fats: 16.8 grams
- ✓ Saturated Fats: 1.2 grams
- ✓ Sugar: 8.7 grams

✓ Fiber .5 grams

✓ Calories: 313

Directions:

- Add 1 cup of water as well as the beef to a slow cooker and let them cook, covered, on a low setting for 6 hours.

1. Once the ingredients are done cooking, discard the bones and add everything else to a blender and blend well prior to serving.

2. At the 5 hour mark, start to prepare the barbeque sauce by taking a saucepan and adding gin the cayenne, paprika, garlic powder, onion powder, Worcestershire sauce, hot sauce, brown sugar, yellow mustard, ketchup and apple cider vinegar and mixing well before placing it on top of a burner over a stove set to a high heat.

3. Let the sauce boil 5 minutes, regularly stirring.

4. After the slow cooker, has finished cooking the beef, remove it and drain the slow cooker before adding in the beef as well as 60 percent of the sauce.

5. Cook everything for 30 minutes on a high heat and top with the remaining sauce prior to serving.

Delicious Slow Cooker Stew

Serving Size: 1

Servings per Recipe: 4

Smart Points per Serving: 7

Calories: 290

Cooking Time: Approx. 6 Hours

Ingredients:

- Beef broth (8 cups)
- Garlic (4 cloves minced)
- Onion (1 large, chopped)
- Carrots (4 medium peeled, chopped)
- Potatoes (4 peeled, chopped)
- Chuck roast (2 lbs. beef, cubed)
- Ground black pepper (as needed)
- Sea salt (to taste)
- Celery (4 stalks chopped)

Nutrition Information:

- ✓ Protein: 27 grams
- ✓ Carbs: 20 grams
- ✓ Fats: 11 grams
- ✓ Saturated Fats: 3 grams
- ✓ Sugar: 3 grams
- ✓ Fiber 3 grams
- ✓ Calories: 290

Directions:

1. Add all of the ingredients, except for the celery to a slow cooker and let them cook, covered, on a high setting for 6 hours.

2. 20 minutes before the stew is done cooking, add in the celery.

3. Serve and enjoy!

White Cheddar Broccoli Mac & Cheese:

Serving Size: 1

Servings per Recipe: 4

Smart Points per Serving: 13

Calories: 387

Cooking Time: Approx. 2 Hours

Ingredients:

- 1/2 cups milk

- 2 egg whites

- 2 teaspoons cornstarch or custard starch

- 1/8 teaspoon nutmeg

- 1 cup ground white cheddar

- 1 little head of broccoli, cut into nibble measured florets

- 2 cups dry, entire wheat pasta

Nutrition Information:

- ✓ Saturated Fat: 7g

- ✓ Cholesterol: 38mg

- ✓ Sodium: 285mg

- ✓ Carbohydrates: 48g

✓ Sugar: 7g

✓ Protein: 21g

Directions:

1. Whisk together the milk, egg whites and cornstarch in the cooker embeds. Make certain to whisk well.

2. Blend in the ground cheddar, broccoli and pasta shells.

3. Cook on low for 1-1/2 to 2 hours.

4. After the main hour, mix the sustenance on a semi-consistent premise.

5. This will do two things. It will permit the pasta to cook equally.

6. It will likewise permit you to watch out for the pasta and see when it's set.

7. Each moderate cooker is distinctive, so the planning for this formula might be marginally unique on this for you.

8. Pasta goes from "cooked" to "mush" rapidly.

9. So make certain to continue mixing every so often to watch out for things.

Slow Cooker Tacos

Serving Size: 2

Servings per Recipe: 8

Smart Points per Serving: 8

Calories: 288

Cooking Time: Approx. 6 Hours

Ingredients:

- 6 inch tortillas (8)
- Bay leaves (2)
- Ground black pepper (to taste)
- Thyme (.25 tsp. dried)
- Cilantro (1 cup chopped)
- Cayenne pepper (.25 tsp.)
- Cinnamon (.5 tsp.)
- Cumin (.5 tsp. ground)
- Chuck roast (2 lbs. beef, cubed)
- Garlic (8 cloves minced)
- Onion (1 chopped)
- Tomatoes (2 chopped)
- 2 jalapeno peppers (chopped, seeded)
- Oil (1 T)

Nutrition Information:

- ✓ Protein: 19 grams
- ✓ Carbs: 15 grams
- ✓ Fats: 17 grams
- ✓ Saturated Fats: 2.1 gram

- ✓ Sugar: .5 grams

- ✓ Fiber 2 grams

- ✓ Calories: 288

Directions:

1. Add the oil to a skillet and place it on the stove over a burner set to a medium/high heat.

2. Add in the garlic as well as the onion, tomatoes and peppers and let them cook for 5 minutes before removing them from the pan and adding them to a blender with 1 tsp. salt and .5 cups water and blend well.

3. Add the results back into the skillet before mixing in the beef and turning the burner to medium and let it brown.

4. Mix in the cayenne pepper, cinnamon and cumin and let everything cook for an additional minute.

5. As this cooks, add 1.5 cups of water as well as the thyme and cilantro into the blender and blend well.

6. Add all of the ingredients to the slow cooker and let them cook, covered, on a low heat for 6 hours.

7. Discard the bay leaves prior to adding the ingredients to the tortillas and serving.

Mushrooms Beef Tips Over Noodles

Serving Size: 1

Servings per Recipe: 4

Smart Points per Serving: 10

Calories: 364

Cooking Time: Approx. 6 Hours

Ingredients:

- Egg noodles (2 cups cooked)
- Water (.25 cups cold)
- Cornstarch (2 T)
- Worcestershire sauce (1 T)
- Beef broth (2 cups)
- Red wine (.3 cups)
- Olive oil (2 tsp.)
- Salt (.5 tsp.)
- Beef tips (1 lb.)
- Onion (1 sliced, halved)
- Mushrooms (.5 lbs.)

Nutrition Information:

- ✓ Protein: 29 grams
- ✓ Carbs: 29 grams
- ✓ Fats: 11.8 grams
- ✓ Saturated Fats: 6.9 grams
- ✓ Sugar: 2 grams
- ✓ Fiber 1 grams

✓ Calories: 364

Directions:

1. Place the onion and the mushrooms into the slow cooker.

2. Season the meet as needed before placing it, along with the oil, into a skillet before placing the skillet onto the stove on top of a burner set to a high/medium heat.

3. Let the meat brown before adding it into the slow cooker.

4. Ensure the skillet is deglazed before adding in the Worcestershire sauce as well as the broth and mixing well.

5. Add the results to the slower cooker and let everything cook on a low heat for 6 hours.

6. Combine the water and cornstarch, add the results to the slow cooker and let everything cook on high for 15 minutes.

7. Plate the noodles and top with the beef tip mixture prior to serving.

One Pot Beef Ragu

Serving Size: 1

Servings per Recipe: 10

Smart Points per Serving: 5

Calories: 224

Cooking Time: Approx. 8 Hours

Ingredients:

- Thyme (2 T chopped)

- Rosemary (2 T chopped)

- Bay leaves (2)

- Beef broth (1.5 cups)

- Tomatoes (14.5 oz. crushed)

- Tomatoes (14.5 oz. diced)

- Garlic (4 cloves minced)

- Carrot (1 diced)

- Onion (.5 diced)

- Celery (1 rib diced)

- Lean been (2.5 lbs.)

Nutrition Information:

- ✓ Protein: 29 grams

- ✓ Carbs: 6 grams

- ✓ Fats: 9 grams

- ✓ Saturated Fats: 4 grams

- ✓ Sugar: 3 grams

- ✓ Fiber 2 grams

- ✓ Calories: 224

Directions:

1. Add all of the ingredients to the slow cooker before covering it, setting it to a low temperature and letting it cook for eight hours.

Slow Cook Beef Lasagna

Serving Size: 2

Servings per Recipe: 6

Smart Points per Serving: 11

Calories: 360

Cooking Time: Approx. 6 Hours

Ingredients:

- Parmesan cheese (.5 cups shredded)
- Lasagna noodles (6)
- Mozzarella cheese (1.5 cups shredded)
- Ricotta cheese (1 cup)
- Red pepper flakes (.25 tsp.)
- Basil (.5 tsp. dried)
- Oregano (1 tsp. dried)
- Salt (1 tsp.)
- Tomato sauce (15 oz.)
- Tomato (28 oz. crushed)
- Garlic (1 clove minced)
- Onion (1 chopped)
- Ground beef (1 lb.)

Nutrition Information:

- ✓ Protein: 28 grams
- ✓ Carbs: 31 grams
- ✓ Fats: 14 grams
- ✓ Saturated Fats: 7 grams
- ✓ Sugar: 2 grams
- ✓ Fiber 1 grams
- ✓ Calories: 360

Directions:

1. Place a skillet on the stove on top of a burner set to a high/medium heat before adding in the garlic, onion and beef and letting the beef brown.

2. Add in the red pepper flakes, basil, oregano, salt, tomato sauce and crushed tomatoes and let the results simmer 5 minutes.

3. Combine the mozzarella and the ricotta cheese.

4. Add .3 of the total sauce from the skillet and add it to the slow cooker. Place 3 noodles on top of the sauce, followed by cheese mixture. Create three layers total.

5. Cover the slow cooker and let it cook on a low heat for 6 hours.

Delicious Mexican Meatloaf:

Serving Size: 1-inch thick slice

Servings per Recipe: 6

Smart Points per Serving: 9

Calories: 335

Cooking Time: Approx. 6 Hours

Ingredients:

For Meatloaf:

- 2 tablespoons olive oil
- 1 onion, slashed
- 1 jalapeño, minced
- 1 clove garlic, minced
- 1 pound ground hamburger
- 1 teaspoon ground cumin
- 1/4 teaspoon cayenne pepper
- 1/2 teaspoon ocean salt
- 1/4 teaspoon dark pepper
- 1/2 cup moved oats, coarsely ground in a sustenance processor
- 1 egg

For Coat:

- 1 cup diced tomatoes in juice
- 1 clove garlic, minced
- 1 tablespoon nectar
- 1 tablespoon lime juice

- 1 canned chipotle stew in adobo sauce

- 1/4 teaspoon Kosher salt

Nutrition Information:

- ✓ Saturated Fat: 3 g

- ✓ Cholesterol: 111mg

- ✓ Sodium: 534 mg

- ✓ Carbohydrates: 12 g

- ✓ Sugars: 5 g

- ✓ Protein: 30 g

Directions:

1. Warm a skillet over medium warmth. Include the olive oil, onions, and jalapeño.

2. Cook until delicate and include the garlic. Cook for 1 moment and add to a huge bowl.

3. Blend in the hamburger and seasonings and blend well. At the point when the blend is marginally cool, include the oats and egg.

4. Shape the blend into a round chunk and exchange to a moderate cooker pot. Cover and cook on low, for 6 hours.

5. Before serving, make the coating by consolidating the greater part of the fixings in a little pan. Heat until it starts boiling.

6. Cook for 5 minutes and exchange to a blender. Mix until smooth.

7. Spoon the meatloaf before serving.

Asian Taste Chicken Curry:

Serving Size: 1 cup

Servings per Recipe: 6

Smart Points per Serving: 11

Calories: 309

Cooking Time: Approx. 4 Hours

Ingredients:

*   1 pound boneless skinless chicken, cut into bite-size pieces

- 1 medium onion daintily cut

- 1 (15 ounces) can chickpeas

- 4-6 little red potatoes, cubed

- 4 medium carrots, chopped

- 1/2 cups coconut milk

- 1/2 cup chicken stock

- 3-4 extensive tomatoes, cleaved

- 2 tablespoons tomato puree

- 2 tablespoons curry powder

- 2 teaspoons salt

- 1/2 teaspoon cayenne pepper

- 1/2 teaspoon ground cumin

- 1 cup green peas, solidified

- 2 tablespoons lemon juice

- 1 teaspoon new ground ginger

- 1/4 cup chopped cilantro, discretionary

Nutrition Information:

- ✓ Saturated Fat: 8 g

- ✓ Cholesterol: 0 mg

- ✓ Sodium: 543 mg

- ✓ Carbohydrates: 39 g

- ✓ Sugars: 6 g

✓ Protein: 18 g

Directions:

1. Least moderate cooker estimate: 5 Quarts

2. Combine coconut milk, chicken stock, tomato puree, curry powder, salt, cumin, and cayenne.

3. Include chicken bosoms, onion, chickpeas, carrots, tomatoes, and potatoes. Cook on high for 4 hours.

4. Include solidified peas, lemon juice, and crisp ginger amid the most recent 10 minutes of cooking.

5. On the other hand, on the off chance that you don't plan to serve immediately include these last ingredients while the ease back cooker is set to warm.

Slow Cook Beef Chili

Serving Size: 1

Servings per Recipe: 12

Smart Points per Serving: 4

Calories: 138

Cooking Time: Approx. 5 Hours

Ingredients:

- Ground black pepper (to taste)

- Sea salt (to taste)

- Tomato paste (2 T)

- Green chilies (.25 cups diced)

- Sweet onion (1 chopped)

- Kidney beans (15 oz. rinsed, drained)

- Tomatoes (28 oz. crushed)

- Cumin (2 tsp.)

- Chili powder (2 T)

- Green bell pepper (1 diced, seeded)

- Red bell pepper (1 diced, seeded)

- Garlic (1 T minced)

- Ground beef (1 lb.)

Nutrition Information:

- ✓ Protein: 13 grams

- ✓ Carbs: 17 grams

- ✓ Fats: 3 grams

- ✓ Saturated Fats: 1 grams

- ✓ Sugar: 2 grams

- ✓ Fiber 5 grams

- ✓ Calories: 138

Directions:

1. Place a skillet on the stove on top of a burner set to a high/medium heat before adding in the garlic, onion and beef and letting the beef brown.

2. Drain the fat from the pan and return the meet to it before adding in the bell peppers and cooking for 5 minutes prior to seasoning using the cumin and chili powder.

3. Add the tomato paste, green chilies, onion, kidney beans, tomatoes and meat mix into the slow cooker and mix well. Cook on high, covered for 5 hours.

4. Season to taste prior to serving.

Chicken with Mushroom Gravy:

Serving Size: 1

Servings per Recipe: 4

Smart Points per Serving: 10

Calories: 341

Cooking Time: Approx. 4 Hours

Ingredients:

- 1 tablespoon additional virgin olive oil

- 4 cuts without nitrate bacon, diced (we utilized turkey bacon)

- 4 boneless, skinless lean chicken bosom filets

- 16 ounces cut cremini mushrooms

- 1 yellow onion daintily cut into rings

- 2 cloves garlic, minced

- 1/2 teaspoon dark pepper

- 1 teaspoon legitimate or ocean salt

- 1/4 cup new level leaf parsley, slashed

- 1/2 cups chicken soup, low-sodium, sans fat

- 2 tablespoons flour

Nutrition Information:

- ✓ Saturated Fat: 5g

- ✓ Cholesterol: 81mg

- ✓ Sodium: 874mg

- ✓ Carbohydrates: 15g

- ✓ Sugar: 5g

- ✓ Protein: 28g

Directions:

1. Add oil to an extensive skillet, swing to medium-high warmth, include diced bacon and cook until fresh.

2. Exchange to a plate with a paper towel on it. Add chicken to the skillet and burn chicken on both sides just until brilliant cocoa.

3. Remove and put on a paper towel.

4. Diminish warmth to medium-low, add onion to a similar skillet, and sauté until delicate, around 4 minutes.

5. Add chicken to a moderate cooker, and then cover with diced bacon, onion, and remaining ingredients, aside from the flour.

6. Wrap and roast on low temperature for 3 to 4 hours, or on high temperature for 1 to 3 hours, or until the chicken is done and effectively drops with a fork.

7. Expel chicken from moderate cooker and put aside. Add flour to a moderate cooker and race until smooth.

8. Return chicken to moderate cooker and keep cooking until sauce is thick 10-15 minutes.

9. When you add the onion to the skillet, pour in around a 1/4 cup soup to deglaze the dish and get every one of the bits on the base of the container from the chicken and afterward add to the moderate cooker.

Italian Chicken and Sweet Potatoes:

Serving Size: 1 ½ cups

Servings per Recipe: 4

Smart Points per Serving: 10

Calories: 364

Cooking Time: Approx. 4 Hours

Ingredients:

- 4 boneless skinless chicken breasts,
- 8 ounces cremini mushrooms sliced
- 2 cups diced sweet potatoes
- 1/4 cup new lemon juice
- 1/2 cup chicken stock
- 1/4 cup olive oil
- 1 teaspoon dried oregano
- 1 teaspoon dried parsley
- 1 teaspoon dried basil
- 1 teaspoon genuine or ocean salt
- 1/2 teaspoon black pepper
- 1/2 teaspoon onion powder
- 2 garlic cloves, minced

Nutrition Information:

- ✓ Saturated Fat: 2g
- ✓ Cholesterol: 62mg
- ✓ Sodium: 700mg
- ✓ Carbohydrates: 33g

✓ Sugar: 8g

✓ Protein: 24g

Directions:

1. Put the chicken in center of the moderate cooker, and after that put the sweet potatoes on the opposite side of the mushrooms.

2. In another bowl, whisk the rest of the fixings together, then pour over the fixings in the moderate cooker.

3. Cover up and cook on low temperature for 6 to 7 hours or on high flame for 3to 4 hours.

Delicious Tamari Glazed Chicken:

Serving Size: 1

Servings per Recipe: 8

Smart Points per Serving: 5

Calories: 176

Cooking Time: Approx. 6 to 8 Hours

Ingredients:

- 8 boneless chicken thighs, skin removed

- 1 tablespoon Chinese 5-flavor powder

- 1 tablespoon olive oil

- 2 white onions, generally cleaved

- 1 cup low-sodium chicken stock

- 1/3 cup rice vinegar

- 1/3 cup tamari

- 1 tablespoon coconut sugar

- 1 teaspoon red bean stew pieces

- 1 bay leaf

- 1/2 cup pea pods

- 2 scallions cut

Nutrition Information:

- ✓ Saturated Fat: 3g

- ✓ Cholesterol: 43mg

- ✓ Sodium: 714mg

- ✓ Carbohydrates: 7g

- ✓ Sugar: 3g

- ✓ Protein: 14g

Directions:

1. Season the chicken thighs with the Chinese 5-flavor powder.

2. Warm the oil in a substantial skillet over medium-high warmth.

3. Include the chicken and cook until caramelized on both sides, 3-4 minutes.

4. Lay the onions in the base of your moderate cooker pot, and lay the chicken pieces on top.

5. Whisk the juices, vinegar, tamari, coconut sugar, red stew pieces, and bay leaf together and pour over the chicken.

6. Cover up and cook on low temperature for 6 to 8 hours or on high flame for 3 to 4 hours.

7. At the point when the chicken is done, include the pea pods and cook 10 minutes, or until delicate.

8. Serve with the scallions.

Brown Rice and Chicken:

Serving Size: 1 cup

Servings per Recipe: 8

Smart Points per Serving: 7

Calories: 289

Cooking Time: Approx. 6 Hours

Ingredients:

For the Rice:

- 2 cups natural Brown Rice

- 5 cups water

- 1 14.5oz. can natural prepared cut diced tomatoes (don't drain)

- 4 ribs natural celery, flushed and diced

- ½ substantial sweet white onion, slashed

- Sirach hot bean stew sauce

- Natural herb blend (no salt) approx. 2 tablespoon

- ½ to 1 teaspoon cumin

- ½ teaspoon paprika

For the Chicken:

- 4 natural boneless/skinless chicken breasts
- ¼to ½ cup gourmet Yoshida sauce
- Sirach hot bean stew sauce (squirt to cover the highest point of the chicken)
- Substantial sprinkling of natural herb blend (no salt)
- 1 tablespoon pounded red bean stew peppers
- 1 teaspoon cumin
- 1 teaspoon paprika
- ½ teaspoon cayenne pepper (discretionary)
- 2 crisp rosemary sprigs

Nutrition Information:

- ✓ Saturated Fat: 0.8 g
- ✓ Cholesterol: 44 mg
- ✓ Sodium: 53 mg
- ✓ Carbohydrates: 40.5 g
- ✓ Sugars: 2.1 g
- ✓ Protein: 20.8 g

Turkey Lasagna Soup:

Serving Size: 1 cup

Servings per Recipe: 8

Smart Points per Serving: 9

Calories: 314

Cooking Time: Approx. 6 to 8 Hours

Ingredients:

- 1 pound lean ground turkey
- 1 (24 ounces) bump tomato basil marinara, no sugar included
- 4 cups chicken juices, low-sodium
- 8 sprigs new (wavy or level) parsley
- 1/2 teaspoon legitimate or ocean salt
- 1/2 teaspoon black pepper
- 8 entire wheat lasagna noodles, broken into fourths
- 1 cup (part-skim) mozzarella cheddar
- 1/2 cup ricotta cheddar, decreased fat
- New basil for trimming, discretionary

Nutrition Information:

- ✓ Saturated Fat: 5g
- ✓ Cholesterol: 66mg
- ✓ Sodium: 336
- ✓ Carbohydrates: 28g

✓ Sugars: 3g

✓ Protein: 25g

Directions:

1. In a skillet over medium warmth, cook ground turkey, parting ways with a fork.

2. Cook only until there's no pink. Deplete off any fat.

3. Add to the moderate cooker, cooked ground turkey, marinara, chicken juices, parsley sprigs, salt, and pepper.

4. Cover and cook on low 4-6 hours. The most recent 30 minutes of cooking time, include broken lasagna noodles, mozzarella.

5. Check noodles to ensure they are delicate, however not soft. Evacuate parsley sprigs before serving, if fancied.

6. Serve in dishes with a touch of ricotta cheddar and trimming with crisp basil, if fancied.

Beef Bourguignon Stew:

Serving Size: 1 cup

Servings per Recipe: 8

Smart Points per Serving: 8

Calories: 310

Cooking Time: Approx. 6 Hours

Ingredients:

- 1/2 pounds lean hamburger hurl, cut into chomp measure solid shapes

- 1 pound reddish brown (Idaho) potatoes, peeled and cleaved into extensive blocks

- 2 carrots, cleaved into 1/2 inch thick cuts

- 2 stalks celery thickly cut

- 3 tablespoons additional virgin olive oil, partitioned

- 1 entire sprig rosemary

- 1 teaspoon dry oregano

- 1 pound white catch mushrooms, divided

- 3 thyme sprigs

- 1 bay leaf

- 2 cloves garlic, minced

- 3 tablespoons white entire wheat flour or universally handy flour

- 1 cup low-sodium hamburger stock

- 3 cups pinot noir

- 10 pearl onions, divided or 1 medium yellow or white onion, diced

- 1 teaspoon fit or sea salt

- 1/2 teaspoon black pepper

Nutrition Information:

- ✓ Saturated Fat: 2g

- ✓ Cholesterol: 54mg

- ✓ Sodium: 141mg

✓ Carbohydrates: 19g

✓ Sugars: 3g

✓ Protein: 23g

Directions:

1. Sprinkle hamburger 3D squares with 1/2 teaspoon salt and 1/2 teaspoon pepper. Dig in flour to coat.

2. Put 1/2 tablespoon of olive oil in the skillet over medium-high warmth.

3. Include a large portion of the meat 3D shapes and chestnut on all sides, for around 5 minutes.

4. It is not important to cook the hamburger completely through, simply burn the exterior.

5. Rehash with the second bunch. Put the hamburger aside.

6. In a similar container that the hamburger was cooked in, include 1/4 cup of the wine and rub the base, permitting a portion of the fluid to vanish.

7. Include herbs, mushrooms, pearl onions or diced onion, celery, carrots, and 1 more tablespoon of olive oil and cook for around 5 minutes.

8. Include garlic and cook for an extra 30 seconds.

9. Empty everything from the dish into the moderate cooker. Include whatever is left of the wine, the stock, whatever is left of the salt, the bay leaf, the potatoes, and meat solid shapes.

10. Cover up and cook on low temperature for 6 to 8 hours or on high flame for 3 to 4 hours.

Slow Cook Fiesta Chili Supper:

Serving Size: 1 cup

Servings per Recipe: 6

Smart Points per Serving: 7

Calories: 254

Cooking Time: Approx. 6 Hours

Ingredients:

- 1 pound lean ground turkey
- 1 (15 ounces) can red kidney beans, depleted and flushed
- 1 clove garlic, minced
- 1/2 cup slashed onion
- 3 cups low sodium chicken or vegetable juices
- 1/2 cups solidified corn bits
- 1/2 cup diced red ringer pepper
- 2 tablespoons bean stew powder, in addition to additional to taste
- 1 teaspoon cumin
- 1 chipotle chili (from can), minced with seeds, in addition to 2 tablespoons sauce from can
- 1 lime, cut into wedges, for serving
- 1/2 teaspoon fit or ocean salt
- 1/2 teaspoon black pepper

Nutrition Information:

- ✓ Saturated Fat: 2g
- ✓ Cholesterol: 56mg

- ✓ Sodium: 459mg

- ✓ Carbohydrates: 24g

- ✓ Sugar: 5g

- ✓ Protein: 22g

Directions:

1. In a medium skillet cook ground turkey just until it loses its pink shading.

2. Get rid of any fat and add to the moderate cooker.

3. Add every single outstanding fixing to the moderate cooker and cook on low for 6 to 8 hours.

4. Present with lime wedges to crush into a stew, if needed.

5. Discretionary fixing thoughts incorporate nonfat sharp cream or Greek yogurt, cleaved cilantro, or scallions.

<u>Vegetarian Enchiladas:</u>

Serving Size: 3

Servings per Recipe: 12

Smart Points per Serving: 13

Calories: 464

Cooking Time: Approx. 4 to 6 Hours

Ingredients:

For Sauce:

- 2 tablespoons olive oil
- 2 tablespoons flour
- 1/4 cup bean stew powder
- 1/2 teaspoon garlic powder
- 1/2 teaspoon salt
- 1/4 teaspoon ground cumin
- 1/4 teaspoon Mexican oregano
- 2 cups vegetable stock

For Enchiladas:

- 1 tablespoon olive oil
- 1 onion, diced
- 1 cup cooked dark beans
- 1/4 cup cleaved new cilantro
- Juice of 1 lime
- 12 corn tortillas
- 1 cup lessened fat destroyed cheddar, separated down the middle
- Lessened fat sharp cream and new hacked cilantro, for serving

Nutrition Information:

- ✓ Saturated Fat: 2 g
- ✓ Cholesterol: 0mg
- ✓ Sodium: 405 mg
- ✓ Carbohydrates: 72 g
- ✓ Sugars: 3 g
- ✓ Protein: 16 g

Directions:

1. Make the sauce by warming a medium pan over medium warmth. Include the olive oil and flour and mix until smooth and bubbly.

2. Include the seasonings and mix until all around joined. Add the stock and heat to the point of boiling.

3. Lessen warmth and stew for 5 minutes.

4. Make the enchilada filling by warming a huge skillet over medium-high warmth. Include the olive oil, trailed by the onions.

5. Cook until the onions are delicate, season with salt and pepper, and include the beans.

6. Cook for around 2 minutes and include the cilantro and lime juice. Kill warm.

7. To make the enchiladas, put the corn tortillas on a plate and cover with a moist paper towel.

8. Microwave for 1 minute, or until tortillas are delicate and malleable.

9. Fill every tortilla with around 2 tablespoons of filling and top with a sprinkling of cheddar.

10. Move up and lay in your moderate cooker, pressing them in firmly so they remain together.

11. On the off chance that the tortillas cool, you may need to warm them.

12. When the greater part of the enchiladas is in the cooker, pour the sauce over top of them, ensuring they are very much secured.

13. Cover and cook on low warmth for 4 6 hours. Before serving, sprinkle remaining cheddar on top, cover, and cook on low for 15 minutes, or until cheddar is liquefied.

14. Present with sharp cream and new cleaved cilantro.

Jambalaya with Chicken and Shrimp:

Serving Size: 1 ½ cups

Servings per Recipe: 4

Smart Points per Serving: 12

Calories: 465

Cooking Time: Approx. 8 Hours

Ingredients:

- 1 pound chicken breasts, cut into bite estimated pieces
- 1 onion, diced
- 1 green pepper, diced
- 4 stalks celery, diced
- 1 cup custom made chicken stock
- 1 tablespoons dried oregano
- 1 tablespoons Cajun or Creole flavoring
- 1 teaspoon hot sauce, or more to taste
- 1 teaspoon dried thyme
- 1 bay leaf
- 1 (28 ounces) can diced tomatoes

- 1 pound peeled and deveined shrimp, tails removed

- 2 cups cooked chestnut rice

- Kosher salt and new ground black pepper, to taste

- New cleaved parsley, for embellishment

Nutrition Information:

- ✓ Saturated Fat: 3 g

- ✓ Cholesterol: 101

- ✓ Sodium: 1125 mg

- ✓ Carbohydrates: 50 g

- ✓ Sugars: 8 g

- ✓ Protein: 40 g

Directions:

1. Consolidate everything aside from the shrimp, rice, and parsley in the moderate cooker.

2. Cook over low warmth for 8 hours.

3. Add the shrimp into the pan, fry for 20 minutes in anticipation of suitable for eating.

4. Serve over the rice with newly slashed parsley on top.

Slow Cook Lasagna Turkey:

Serving Size: 1 slice

Servings per Recipe: 8

Smart Points per Serving: 6

Calories: 199

Cooking Time: Approx. 6 Hours

Ingredients:

- 1 pound lean ground turkey, or lean ground hamburger

- 1 vast onion, diced

- 3 cloves garlic, minced

- 2 (25 ounces) cups pasta sauce, no sugar included

- 2 cups low-fat curds

- 8 ounces destroyed (part skim) mozzarella cheddar

- 1 teaspoon Italian flavoring

- Squeeze of salt

- 12 (uncooked) entire wheat lasagna noodles, (soften up half before adding to moderate cooker)

- 1/2 cup naturally ground Parmesan cheddar

- Crisp basil, for enhancement

Nutrition Information:

- ✓ Saturated Fat: 5 g

- ✓ Cholesterol: 78

- ✓ Sodium: 1015 mg

- ✓ Carbohydrates: 33 g

- ✓ Sugars: 8 g
- ✓ Protein: 38 g

Directions:

1. Add the turkey and onion to a huge skillet and cook over medium warmth until the turkey has lost its pink shading.

2. Include the garlic and cook for one extra moment. Empty any fat out of the cooked turkey.

3. Include 1/2 cup pasta sauce and mix to join.

4. Join the curds, mozzarella, Italian flavoring, and salt.

5. Include a 1/2 cup meat sauce to the base of the moderate cooker. Next, include a layer of lasagna noodles and spread 1/4 cheddar blend over noodles.

6. Rehash the layers until these fixings are no more.

7. Cover and cook in the moderate cooker on low warmth until noodles are still somewhat firm and cheddar is bubbly roughly 4-6 hours.

8. Evacuate the top and add the parmesan to the top. Kill the moderate cooker and permit the goulash to sit for 15 minutes before cutting.

9. In the event that coveted, serve decorated with the crisp basil and extra parmesan.

Vegetarian Recipes

Black Bean Enchiladas & Spinach

Each serving contains
- Protein: 26 grams
- Carbs: 30 grams
- Fats: 5 grams
- Saturated Fats: 3 grams

- Sugar: 7 grams
- Fiber 10 grams
- Calories: 217

Smart Points: 7

What to Use
- Ground black pepper (to taste)
- Sea salt (to taste)
- Lime juice (1 lime)
- Chili powder (1 tsp.)
- Coriander (1 tsp. ground)
- Cumin (1 tsp. ground)
- Sharp cheddar cheese
- Sour cream (.5 cups)
- Salsa Verde (24 oz.)
- Whole wheat tortilla (8)
- Corn (1 cup)
- Black beans
- Spinach

What to Do
- Place half the total number of black beans in a large bowl and mash them prior to adding in the pepper, salt, lime juice, chili powder, coriander, cumin, other black beans, corn and spinach and mix well.
- Add half of the salsa to the slow cooker before adding the bean mixture to each tortilla and rolling tightly. Ideally all of the rolled tortillas will fit in a single layer in the slow cooker.
- Add in the rest of the salsa along with the cheese and let everything cook, covered, on a low setting for 3 hours.
- Top with jalapenos, onions, cilantro and sour cream prior to serving.

One Pot Pea Carrot Soup

Each serving contains

- Protein: 8.3 grams
- Carbs: 7.7 grams
- Fats: 2 grams
- Saturated Fats: 1 gram
- Sugar: 3 grams
- Fiber 2 grams
- Calories: 85

Smart Points: 2

What to Use
- Carrot (1 cup chopped)
- Garlic (1 T minced)
- Onion (.5 cups chopped fine)
- Vegetable broth (8 cups)
- Split peas (16 oz. dried)

What to Do
- Add all of the ingredients to a slow cooker and let them cook, covered, on a high setting for 6 hours.
- Once the ingredients are done cooking add everything else to a blender and blend well prior to serving.

Slow Cook Vegies Casserole

Each serving contains
- Protein: 24 grams
- Carbs: 16 grams
- Fats: 8 grams
- Saturated Fats: 3.4 grams
- Sugar: 2 grams
- Fiber 2 grams
- Calories: 245

Smart Points: 6

What to Use
- Ground black pepper (to taste)
- Sea salt (to taste)
- Dry mustard (.5 tsp.)
- Paprika (.5 tsp.)
- Pepper (.5 tsp.)
- Garlic powder (1 tsp.)
- Scallions (6 diced)
- Fat free milk (1 cup)
- Egg whites (14)
- Mushrooms (8 oz. diced)
- Bell pepper (1 diced)
- Cheddar cheese (1 cup shredded)
- Hash browns (1 packaged frozen)

What to Do
- Ensure the slow cooker has been sprayed down using cooking spray to ensure nothing sticks.
- Layer in the mushrooms, onions, bell peppers and potatoes plus the cheese so that it makes two or three distinct layers.
- Combine the dry mustard, garlic powder, paprika, pepper, salt, milk and egg whites together in a mixing bowl and mix well before adding the results to the slow cooker.
- Cover the slow cooker and let it cook on a low heat for 6 hours.

Lentil & Pumpkin Stew

Each serving contains
- Protein: 11 grams
- Carbs: 32 grams
- Fats: 0 grams
- Saturated Fats: 0 grams
- Sugar: .5 grams
- Fiber 10 grams
- Calories: 173

Smart Points: 4

What to Use
- Ground black pepper (to taste)
- Sea salt (to taste)
- Cilantro (1 handful chopped)
- Plain Greek yogurt (.5 cups)
- Nutmeg (1 tsp.)
- Turmeric (1 tsp.)
- Ginger (1 T ground)
- Cumin (1 T ground)
- Lime juice (1 lime)
- Tomato paste (2 To
- Vegetable broth (4 cups)
- Onion (1 chopped fine)
- Green lentils (1 cup)
- Pumpkin (2 lbs. cubed)

What to Do
- Add the pepper, salt, nutmeg, turmeric, ginger, cumin, lime juice, tomato paste, vegetable broth, onion, green lentils and pumpkin to the slow cooker.
- Cover the slow cooker and let it cook on a low heat for 6 hours.

Top each serving with plain Greek yogurt and cilantro prior to serving.

One Pot Vegetable Soup

Each serving contains
- Protein: 4 grams
- Carbs: 28 grams
- Fats: 2 grams
- Saturated Fats: 1 gram
- Sugar: 9 grams
- Fiber 7 grams
- Calories: 131

Smart Points: 5

What to Use
- Water (2 cups)
- Vegetable broth (6 cups)
- Salt (1.25 tsp.)
- Cinnamon (2 sticks)
- Ginger (1 T minced)
- Brown Sugar (2 T)
- Onions (2 sliced)
- Olive oil (2 T)
- Butternut squash (6 lbs. sliced)

What to Do
- Start by making sure your oven is heated to 350 degrees F.
- Place the squash halves onto a baking sheet before placing the sheet in the oven and letting it cook 15 minutes. After it has finished baking, remove it from the stove to allow it to cool.
- As the squash cools, place a pan on the oven over a medium/high heat add in the oil and the onion and let it cook for 3 minutes before adding in the garlic, ginger and brown sugar and letting everything cook for an additional minute.
- Add the results to a slow cooker and let them cook, covered, on a low setting for 6 hours.
- Once the ingredients are done cooking, discard the cinnamon sticks and add everything else to a blender and blend well prior to serving.

Slow Cook Potato Chowder

Each serving contains
- Protein: 9 grams
- Carbs: 28 grams
- Fats: 2.8 grams
- Saturated Fats: .5 grams

- Sugar: 1.5 grams
- Fiber 4 grams
- Calories: 170

Smart Points: 4

What to Use
- Half and half (1 cup)
- Thyme (.25 tsp. crushed)
- Bay leaf (1)
- Barley (.5 cups)
- Vegetable broth (4 cups)
- Garlic (3 cloves minced)
- Leeks (1 cup chopped)
- Carrot (1 diced)
- Potatoes (2 cups cubes)

What to Do
- Place all of the ingredients expect for the half and half into the slow cooker, cover it, and let it cook on a low heat for 6 hours.
- 10 minutes prior to serving, and in the half and half and let it heat, uncovered for 10 minutes.

Delicious Minestrone Soup

Each serving contains
- Protein: 2 grams
- Carbs: 17 grams
- Fats: 3 grams
- Saturated Fats: 1 grams
- Sugar: 2 grams
- Fiber 5 grams
- Calories: 250

Smart Points: 5

What to Use

- Ground black pepper (to taste)
- Sea salt (to taste)
- Parmesan cheese (3 T)
- Extra virgin olive oil (2 T)
- Potato (1 lb., diced, peeled)
- Green beans (1.5 cups chopped)
- Zucchini (1 quartered)
- Leek (1 chopped)
- Celery (1 stalk diced)
- Carrot (1 diced)
- Cannellini beans (19 oz.)
- Tomatoes (14.5 oz. diced)
- Vegetable broth (4 cups)

What to Do
- Add all of the ingredients except for the cheese into the slow cooker and cook, covered, on a low heat for 6 hours.
- Add the parmesan cheese prior to serving.

Slow Cook French Onion Soup

Each serving contains
- Protein: 15 grams
- Carbs: 53 grams
- Fats: 8 grams
- Saturated Fats: 3 grams
- Sugar: 8 grams
- Fiber 4 grams
- Calories: 331

Smart Points: 10

What to Use
- French bread (6 slices)
- Ground black pepper (to taste)
- Sea salt (to taste)

- Goat cheese (2 oz.)
- Vegetable broth (6 cups)
- Thyme (.5 tsp crushed)
- Thyme (3 springs)
- All-purpose flour (1 T)
- Onion (3 lbs. sliced)
- Canola oil (1 T)

What to Do
- Add the oil to a Dutch oven and place it over a medium heat. Add in the salt as well as the onion and let it cook for 35 minutes, stirring regularly.
- Add in the flour and let it cook for 2 minutes, stirring as needed.
- Add the onions into the slow cooker before adding in the pepper as well as the sprigs of thyme. Add in the broth and cook, covered, on a low heat for 10 hours.
- Remove the sprigs of time, plate on top of the bread and then top with the remaining ingredients as desired.

Slow Cooker Vegan Risotto

Each serving contains
- Protein: 29 grams
- Carbs: 29 grams
- Fats: 11.8 grams
- Saturated Fats: 6.9 grams
- Sugar: 2 grams
- Fiber 1 grams
- Calories: 364

Smart Points: 10

What to Use
- Ground black pepper (to taste)

- Sea salt (to taste)
- Lemon zest (1 To
- Garlic (3 cloves minced)
- Fennel seeds (2 tsp. crushed)
- Plain Greek Yogurt (.3 cups)
- Parmesan cheese (.5 cups grated)
- Mushrooms (.5 cups chopped)
- Shallot (1 finely chopped)
- Carrot (1 peeled, chopped fine)
- Green onions (.3 cups diced)
- Green beans (2 cups cooked)
- Fennel bulb (1 cored, diced fine)
- Dry white wine (.3 cups)
- Water (1 cup)
- Vegetable broth (3 cups)
- Brown rice (1 cup)

What to Do
- Coat the inside of the slow cooker using cooking spray to keep things from sticking.
- Add the garlic, shallot, carrot, rice, fennel and fennel seeds into the slow cooker before adding in the wine, the water and the broth and stirring well.
- Cover the slow cooker and let it cook on a low heat for 3.5 hours.
- Prior to serving, mix in the pepper, lemon zest, yogurt, parmesan cheese, green onions, mushroom and green beans.

Sweet Potato One Pot Soup

Each serving contains
- Protein: 2 grams
- Carbs: 23 grams
- Fats: 1 gram
- Saturated Fats: 0 grams
- Sugar: 0 grams
- Fiber 2.6 grams

- Calories: 112

Smart Points: 2

What to Use
- Ground black pepper (to taste)
- Sea salt (to taste)
- Dry mustard (1 tsp.)
- Allspice (.5 tsp.)
- Truvia (2 packets)
- Half and half (1.5 cups)
- Sweet potatoes (4 sliced, peeled)
- Vegetable broth (2 cups)

What to Do
- Place the potato slices and the broth into the slow cooker, cover the slow cooker and let it cook on a medium heat for 3 hours.
- Add the results to a food processor and process well.
- Add all of the ingredients to the slow cooker, cover it, and cook at a medium heat for an additional hour.

Slow Cook Snacks Recipes

Delicious Plum Pudding with Fruits

Prep Time: 50 minutes

Cook Time: 4 hours.

Servings: 12

Points: 7

INGREDIENTS

Fruits

- ¾ cup currants
- ¾ cup dried apricot
- ¾ cup dates pitted
- 145 g candied oranges
- ¾ cup orange juice
- 125 ml of masala
- 1 orange, finely grated zest

Cake

- 1 cup almond powder
- 1 tsp. ground cinnamon
- 1 tsp. of five-spices
- 1 tsp. baking powder
- ½ cup butter
- ½ cup brown sugar
- 2 eggs
- 1 ½ cup all-purpose flour

PREPARATION

Fruits

In a medium sized bowl, mix all the INGREDIENTS. Plastic wrap and soak for 12 hours while covered on with a plastic wrap.

Cake

1. Butter your loaf pan and add and line with parchment paper.

2. In a bowl, mix almond powder, spices, flour, and baking powder. Book.

3. In a medium-sized bowl, mix brown sugar and cream butter the electric mixer.

4. Beat the eggs and whisk until the mixture is homogeneous.

5. With a wooden spoon, add drained fruit and dry INGREDIENTS and stir.

6. Divide the dough into the pan and add into a slow cooker. Pour water until halfway up the pan.

7. Cook on low for 4 hours.

Nutrition Information

Calories: 260

Protein: 2g

Fat: 6g

Carbohydrates: 49g

Nice Hot Cider Cranberries

Prep time: 5 minutes

Cooking time: 20 minutes.

Servings: 6

Points: 3

INGREDIENTS

- 2 liters of cranberry juice
- Zest of 2 oranges
- 14 cloves
- 1 1/2 cup dried cranberries
- 1 c. vanilla
- 1 1/3 cup honey
- 2 cinnamon sticks

PREPARATION

1. Pour the cranberry juice into a slow cooker and set on high.

2. Stir in the orange zest, nails, cranberries, vanilla, honey, and cinnamon sticks.

3. Cook, occasionally stirring, until the casserole is heated through, about 20 minutes.

Nutrition Information

Calories: 120

Protein: 0g

Fat: 0g

Carbohydrates: 30g

Heavenly Cocktail Sausages

Prep time: 10 minutes

Cooking time: 2 hours.

Servings: 6

Points: 1

INGREDIENTS

- 2 ¼ cups BBQ sauce
- 1 cup packed brown sugar
- 1/2 cup ketchup
- 1 c. tablespoon Worcestershire sauce
- 1/3 cup chopped onion
- 4 packages (225 g each) cocktail sausages

PREPARATION

1. Combine and mix all INGREDIENTS in the bowl of slow cooker. Cook on low for 2 hours.

Nutrition Information

Calories: 21

Protein: 0.9g

Fat: 1.4g

Carbohydrates: 1g

Refreshing Herbal Composite

Prep Time: 10 minutes

Cook Time: 4hours.

Servings: 6

Points: 8

INGREDIENTS

- 3 cups brown lentils
- 1/4 cup chopped fresh parsley
- 1/4 cup curry paste
- 1 c. grated ginger
- 2 c. tablespoons chopped fresh oregano
- 2 cloves garlic, minced
- 1 c. tablespoons all-purpose flour

- 1 c. to paprika

PREPARATION

1. Combine all INGREDIENTS in the bowl of a slow cooker 5 liters capacity; mix.

2. Add water up to ½ inch from the edge. Cover and cook on high (HIGH) for 4 hours.

Nutrition Information

Calories: 317

Protein: 21g

Fat: 6g

Carbohydrates: 46g

Slow Cook Chocolate Pudding

Prep Time: 30 minutes

Cook Time: 2 hours.

Servings: 8

Points: 6

INGREDIENTS

Sauce

- 2 1/4 cups brown sugar
- 1/2 cup cocoa, sifted
- 1 tbsp. cornstarch
- 4 oz. dark chocolate, coarsely chopped
- 1 1/2 cup water
- 1 1/2 cup of 35%, 15% or 5% cooking cream
- 1/2 tsp. vanilla extract

Cake

- 1 1/2 cup of all-purpose flour
- 1/2 tsp. of baking soda
- a pinch of salt
- 3/4 cup butter
- 1/2 tsp. baking powder
- 1/3 cup cocoa, sifted
- 1 egg
- 1 egg yolk
- 1 cup sugar
- 3/4 cup milk

PREPARATION

Sauce

1. Combine cocoa, brown sugar, and starch in a saucepan. Add remaining INGREDIENTS. Bring to a boil, stirring with a whisk and simmer for 10 seconds. Transfer to slow cooker.

Cake

1. Combine flour, baking soda, baking powder, and salt in a bowl. Set aside.

2. Again, combine sugar and cocoa with cream butter with an electric mixer.

3. Beat the eggs into the mixture and beat until you obtain a homogenous.

4. Slowly add the all your dry INGREDIENTS alternating with the milk.

5. Using a scoop or a large spoon, spread the dough over the hot chocolate sauce.

6. Place a clean cloth over the slow cooker without touching the batter. Cover and cook for 2 hours. Remove container from slow cooker. Remove the lid and let stand for 15 minutes. Serve hot or cold.

Nutrition Information

Calories: 210

Protein: 3g

Fat: 10g

Carbohydrates: 27g

Gratifying Strawberry Pudding

Prep Time: 10 minutes

Cook Time: 2hours.

Servings: 6

Points: 3

INGREDIENTS

- 1 cup flour

- 1/3 cup sugar

- 1 1/2 c. Tea baking powder

- 1/2 c. Tea ground cinnamon

- 1/2 c. Salt tea

- 2 large eggs, beaten with a fork

- 2 c. Oil table

- 3 cups frozen strawberries 1 cup each: raspberries, blueberries, and strawberries

- 1/2 cup granulated sugar

- 1/2 cup water

PREPARATION

1. Combine first 5 INGREDIENTS in a bowl. Stir.

2. Add eggs, oil, milk and vanilla. Mix well.

3. Pour 3.5 liters into a slow cooker

4. Put the last 5 INGREDIENTS in a saucepan.

5. Heat, occasionally stirring until mixture boils.

6. Pour into slow cooker.

7. Put 3 layers of paper towels on top of the slow cooker and cover. Cook for 2 hours at low temperature.

Nutrition Information

Calories: 140

Protein: 7g

Fat: 4.2 g

Carbohydrates: 18g

Sweet Macaroni and Cheese

Prep Time: 10 minutes

Cook Time: 6 hours.

Servings: 6

Points: 5

INGREDIENTS

- 225g uncooked macaroni

- 4 cups Cheddar cheese, grated, divided

- 1 can (370 ml) evaporated milk

- 1 ½ cup milk

- 2 eggs

- 1 c. teaspoon salt

- 1/2 c. pepper tea

PREPARATION

1. Grease the inside of the bowl of the slow cooker with cooking spray and spray.

2. In a large bowl, beat eggs, evaporated milk, and milk. Add uncooked macaroni and 3 cups shredded cheese. Transfer the bowl to the slow cooker. Sprinkle remaining grated cheese on top.

3. Cook on low heat for 5-6 hours.

4. Do not lift the lid during cooking.

Nutrition Information

Calories: 167

Protcin: 10g

Fat: 4.5g

Carbohydrates: 21g

Slow Cook Brown Bread with Raisins

Prep time: 10 minutes

Cooking time: 2 hours

Servings: 3

Points: 3

INGREDIENTS

- 3 cups whole wheat flour
- 1 c. table fills baking powder
- 2 c. table molasses or corn syrup.
- 1/2 c. cinnamon tea
- 1/2 c. nutmeg tea
- 2 c. Oil table
- 1 1/2 cups water or as needed
- 1/2 cup raisins

PREPARATION

1. Combine flour, baking powder, nutmeg, and cinnamon. Add half a cup of raisins.

2. Add the oil, molasses, and water. Stir to moisten.

3. Pour into a well-greased slow cooker container.

4. Place a 5 paper towel between the lid and the container of the slow cooker to absorb excess moisture.

5. Cook over high heat for 1 hour 45 minutes. Do not lift the lid during cooking.

Nutrition Information

Calories: 130

Protein: 3g

Fat: 0g

Carbohydrates: 29g

Fiber: 2g

Tasty Almond Bread

Prep time: 5 minutes

Cooking time: 3 hours

Servings: 4

Points: 4

INGREDIENTS

- 2 cups warm water
- 1 package of active dry yeast
- 1 c table sugar
- 3 1/2 cups plain flour
- 1/2 tsp. teaspoon salt
- 2 tablespoons oil table
- Almond Milk

PREPARATION

1. Preheat slow cooker to HIGH with the lid closed. Dissolve yeast in 1/2 cup warm water with sugar and put in a warm place.

2. Put the flour in a large bowl and sprinkle with salt. Make a well in the center.

3. When yeast is bubbling: put the rest of the water and the add oil into the flour. Stir with your fingers until all the flour is absorbed.

4. Grease a pan and put the bread crumbs.

5. Top with almond milk. Cover with a plate and let stand for 5 minutes in a warm place.

6. Place on a trivet (support) in the crockpot, cover and cook for 2-3 hours.

Nutrition Information

Calories: 160

Protein: 5g

Fat: 4g

Carbohydrates: 26g

Delicious Cinnamon Flavored Oats

Prep time: 5 minutes

Cooking time: 9 hours

Servings: 3

Points: 4

INGREDIENTS

- 2 cups of oatmeal
- 2 apples
- 1 tsp. cinnamon
- 4 cups of water

PREPARATION

1. Pour all INGREDIENTS in a slow cooker. Do NOT stir.
2. Cook overnight for 8 – 9 hours on low.

Nutrition Information

Calories: 160

Protein: 4g

Fat: 2g

Carbohydrates: 32g

Conclusion

Thank you again for downloading this book!

I hope this book was able to help you in creating some amazing slow cooker recipes and your weight loss journey.

The next step is to go and shed some weight using our extra time that we get from an easy cooking lifestyle and the help of your slow cooker.

Finally, if you enjoyed this book, then I'd like to ask you for a favor, would you be kind enough to leave a review for this book on Amazon? It'd be greatly appreciated!

Thank you and good luck!

Wendy Wilson

19296378R00098

Printed in Poland
by Amazon Fulfillment
Poland Sp. z o.o., Wrocław